THE GLASS MENAGERIE

BY TENNESSEE WILLIAMS

Laurette Taylor as Amanda Wingfield in a publicity still from the original
1944 Chicago production of *The Glass Menagerie*.
(*Photo courtesy of the Billy Rose Theatre Division
at the New York Public Library for the Performing Arts.*)

TENNESSEE WILLIAMS

THE GLASS MENAGERIE

DELUXE CENTENNIAL EDITION

INTRODUCTION BY
TONY KUSHNER

A NEW DIRECTIONS BOOK

CONTENTS

INTRODUCTION

Notes on *The Glass Menagerie*

In June of 1943, slightly more than a year before he completed *The Glass Menagerie*, eighteen months before the play premiered in Chicago, a little less than two years before it moved on to New York and "in one stroke," as Arthur Miller later declared, "lifted lyricism to its highest level in our theater's history," Tennessee Williams wrote a short story called "Portrait of a Girl in Glass."

A mere twelve pages in this edition, the story is a prose sketch of the very simple plot of *The Glass Menagerie*. All five of the play's characters are present in the short story—or rather four are present and one, the father, as he is in the play, is an absent presence, or a present absence. The family's name in the story is Wingfield. It's narrated by a poet/shoe warehouse stock boy named Tom, and he has a sister named Laura. Laura's gentleman caller in the story is a Mr. Delaney, while in the play he's O'Connor, a slight variation on Connor, the name of one of Tennessee's Alpha Tau Omega fraternity brothers from his undergraduate days at the University of Missouri. In the story and the play, as it was in the ATO frat house in 1929, his first name is Jim.

The only significant character in "Portrait of a Girl in Glass" who remains unnamed is the narrator's mother. He calls her "Mother," which conveys her son's irritation with her, and even contempt. And in the short story, she's the fourth wheel, less significant to the unfolding action than her children or her dinner guest; the generic title will do.

It's something of a surprise to encounter, in published versions of the play, all the characters labeled thus in the first cast listing—The Mother, Her Daughter, Her Son, and The Gentleman Caller—before a second gives their proper names. This generic catalog of types, preserved, presumably at the playwright's behest, from the cast list in the original production's Playbill, seems consonant with other striking, unexpected gestures in the text of the play toward a non-Naturalistic theater of type and distancation. These gestures—scene titles, slides—are unexpected because they're rarely heeded in production, understandably, since they feel at odds with everything that's made the play so central to the dramatic canon. Given how specific the play's characters are, how indelible they are, listing them as types seems clinical, sterile, wrong, even coy.

Regardless of the way the characters are identified in the program of any production of *The Glass Menagerie*, no matter how ignorant audience members might be of American dramatic literature, they'll learn, when her narrator son, mere minutes into the play, informs them that Mother's given—or perhaps more appropriately, *Christian*—name is Amanda.

Amanda Wingfield heads the parade of Tennessee Williams's great female characters, followed by Blanche DuBois, Maggie the Cat, and the long line of their successors. We think of Amanda as the central role in *Menagerie*, and in many ways she is. She's indisputably the dominant presence onstage, and she dominates by talking. She seems, like Hamlet, to talk nonstop, while the other characters struggle to get a word in edgewise. From the moment Amanda emerges from Tom's memory, in each of *Menagerie*'s seven scenes, she's talking. She's only offstage for any significant period of time during Tom's drunken arrival at the top of Scene Four (the idea for which scene came from the actor Eddie Dowling, the original Tom, and the critic/busybody George Jean Nathan), and during Laura's and Jim's postprandial visit in Scene Seven. Amanda ceases to talk at the play's conclusion, when her son forces her to become a silent, remembered image. Her silence (the stage direction rather jarringly informs us) is an improvement over the flesh-and-blood Amanda: "Now that we cannot hear the mother's speech, her silliness is gone and she has dignity and tragic beauty."

It's jarring to read this because any good actress in the role of Amanda Wingfield will show her audience, along with the character's silliness, along with her exasperating blindness and relentless nagging, the woman's indestructible dignity, her vital wit, her fierce devotion to her children, her tragic relationship to hope, to beauty, and to loss. Any reasonable reading of the text will deliver the same understanding. The playwright's late interjection in the text may have been intended to underscore Amanda's heroism, but it also sounds angrily relieved to have finally managed to shut her up.

Amanda Wingfield, of course, is Edwina Williams, and her son Tom is Thomas Lanier Williams, who, in the process of crafting the person who would craft his plays, rechristened himself Tennessee.

His nom de plume is so firmly fixed in the pantheon, so tamed by familiarity, that it takes an effort to see that choosing that name was a large, daring gesture. "Tennessee" is cannily attention-getting, as it was meant to be, and also of course a disguise, half hayseed (Arthur Miller wrote that when he first heard it, he envisioned someone "in buckskins, carrying a rifle") and half outrageous drag provocation (Dorothy Parker, according to Tennessee's biographer Lyle Leverich, remarked "*Tennessee* Williams! I might as well call myself Palestine Parker!"; Theresa Helburn, administrator of the Theatre Guild, using her married name and the location of her summer home, sometimes signed her letters to Tennessee "Connecticut Opdycke").

The name is also a gesture of identification with his Memphis-born father. This is curious, considering how often in his letters and journals Tennessee declared his dislike of Cornelius Coffin Williams, his contempt for his father's alcohol-fuelled bullying and philistinism. It's a truism, and also true, that the victim of abuse may respond to his abuser with masochistic affection, a self-preservational gambit in desperate circumstances, an attempt to form a connection, any connection, at whatever the cost, to power. In Tennessee's case, the aspect of paternal power that attracted him was only partially the sadist's power to dominate and destroy. Given his father, it's unlikely that there'd be no sadomasochistic residue in Tennessee's psyche, without which (on the bright side!) it's highly unlikely he'd have created Stanley Kowalski. What seems to have appealed most to the young Tennessee is not the pathological strength of the bonds of affection forged by his father's aggression and callousness, but rather the way that Cornelius's brutishness loosened his own feelings of familial attachment, affording him a degree of freedom, a measured power of flight.

Unlike the MIA Wingfield patriarch in both "Portrait" and *Menagerie*, Cornelius stayed with his family, returning after every drunken debauch (it was Edwina who eventually left him). But Tennessee discerned in his father's belligerence a resistance to domesticity, a yearning for escape. This yearning failed to emancipate Cornelius, who lacked a ruthless devotion to an alternative vision of happiness, and the courage and imagination to pursue it, insufficiencies of spirit which far less severely afflicted his son.

This affinity with his father is reflected in the short story and in the play. Tom, in *Menagerie*, tells us nothing about his father apart from his having disappeared. No judgment is rendered, no blame or rage is expressed concerning this man whose abrogation of paternal responsibility has forced his son into drudgery and his family into a hardscrabble, penurious existence. Tom's only expressed feeling about his father is a barely concealed envy of his successful departure and disappearance. He presents his father as a Cheshire Cat who's left behind only his portrait's charming, indecipherable smile.

There's one difference in the way the father is presented in the short story (and having mentioned this, "Portrait" will be set aside for the time being, until it's opportune to consider one last difference, perhaps the most significant difference, between story and play). In "Portrait of a Girl in Glass," the father leaves behind his phonograph and record collection. He vanishes, but he bequeaths to his children the gift of music.

Did Tennessee choose his writing name in acknowledgment of the paternal source of his own literary music? A branch of his father's family tree is adorned by the nineteenth-century poet Sidney Lanier, to whom Tennessee was indebted for his middle name and, to the extent that talent owes anything to genetics, perhaps for some part of his abilities. But it was Cornelius the shoe salesman's lifelong rage against the desk job and the household in which he got miserably stuck that struck a chord of sympathy in Tennessee, who chose to embody and actualize his father's itinerant dreams. If in his christening of his writing self he was identifying with his father's refusal of hearth and home, the choice is also a dis-identification with his Ohio-born mother, a gesture of separation and distance from her. Her Southern melodic prolixity was an important source of his poetry. But he loyalty, faith, affection, material and emotional support—and that unstintingly provided by his devoted maternal grandparents, the Dakins—came at the price of fidelity to something from which Tennessee felt he had to run in order to become a writer. He didn't decide to call himself Ohio Williams.

Gore Vidal, intermittently one of Tennessee's close friends, calls Edwina Williams the first of the "Monster Women" who occupied pride of place in the playwright's life and art. While one hopes that Tennessee would have rejected Vidal's misogynist designation of his mother and the other women who tried to help organize and sometimes commandeer his life, there's no question that he felt profoundly ambivalent about Edwina. In a review of Tennessee's *Memoirs* in *The New York Review of Books*, Vidal recounts a dinner with Mrs. Williams and her son:

> "I had forty gentlemen callers that day," she says, complacently.... Delicately she holds a fork with a shrimp on it. Fork and shrimp proceed slowly to her mouth while Tennessee and I stare, hypnotized not only by the constant flow of conversation but by the never-eaten shrimp for just as she is about to take the first bite, yet another anecdote wells up from deep inside her ... ah, *solipsistic* brain and the fork returns to the plate, the shrimp untouched. "Tom, remember when that little dog took

the hat with the plume and ran with it all 'round the yard?" This is also from *The Glass Menagerie*. Tennessee nervously clears his throat. Again the shrimp rises to the wide straight mouth which resembles nothing so much as the opening to a miniature letter box—one designed for engraved invitations only. But once again the shrimp does not arrive. "Tom, do you remember ...?"

Tennessee clears his throat again. "*Mother, eat your shrimp.*"

"Why," counters Miss Edwina, "do you keep making that funny sound with your throat?"

"Because, Mother, when you destroy someone's life you must expect certain nervous disabilities."

Leaving aside the camp comedy of two gay men sitting transfixed in vaginophobic horror while Mother threatens repeatedly to bite a shrimp in two, Tennessee sounds in Vidal's anecdote a lot like his character Tom, about whose furious anger toward Amanda, as well as his immense, imprisoning devotion, the playwright has permitted no doubt.

The overarching dramatic problem in *The Glass Menagerie*, the conflict that generates the play's quietly unbearable pressure, is the desperate necessity for Tom's psychic survival that he betray, through abandonment, his mother and his sister. He's caught in "a trap," he tells us at the beginning of the play, and to escape he must "act without pity." After the betrayal, abandonment, and liberation, and after a time in exile, adrift, lonely (despite the "companions" he meets along the way), Tom, or rather the playwright for whom he is nakedly the surrogate, will write *The Glass Menagerie*.

The playwright's pre-*Menagerie* exilic period was considerably less forlorn than that described by his character. Tennessee never wandered far from a post office or Western Union storefront at which he might pick up the checks his mother and his maternal grandmother uncomplainingly provided, or remittances from grants and prize money he'd received before his reputation was made, parceled out by his devoted and prescient agent, Audrey Wood. His odyssey through New Orleans, Mexico, the American Southwest, California, and Cape Cod was rough going at times, but hardly the derelict life evoked in Tom's monologues, which somewhat resemble the narration in film noir.

The resemblance is not accidental. *Menagerie* is connected to film noir in a number of ways. The films that established the genre were made in the late 1930s and early '40s, immediately before and during World War II, while Tennessee was at work on *Menagerie*. Most of these films were narrated, as *Menagerie* is, and many are told in flashback, as *Menagerie* is. Tom's monologues are a kind of public confessing, and though he isn't confessing a crime—at least not the kind for which people get arrested—he's a lost soul roaming the nocturnal streets of an unnamed city, sharing with an unseen audience, or with himself, or with God, the guilty thoughts in his head.

In the bifurcated photographic cover of the aforementioned first *Playbill* for *The Glass Menagerie*, Laurette Taylor's legendary Amanda occupies the right side, bowing in her party dress to the memory of a gentleman caller; on the left side is pudgy, fifty-year-old, too-old-for-the-role Eddie Dowling as Tom, smoking, leaning against a fire escape in a merchant marine's wool cap and peacoat, looking not a bit like the tender young poet haunted by the soulful, sad, oddly dressed woman on the right—looking, in fact, much more like a grizzled waterfront vagrant from *The Maltese Falcon*.

Tom's cadences, fluid and tender, are more obviously indebted to Keats, Whitman, and Hart Crane than to the hard-bitten sounds of James M. Cain and Raymond Chandler, or to the screenplays derived from their novels. But the best of their work has an overwhelming, elegiac musicality, an electricity, and most importantly a poetic reach in their grittily lyrical prose that makes it plausible to propose noir as a significant antecedent to the breakthroughs that allowed Tennessee to write his first great play—and more than that, to suggest that he was possessed of ambitions similar to the writers who created noir.

Writers like Cain and especially Chandler transformed popular art forms—the detective novel and its cinematic equivalent, which were traditionally and possibly essentially grounded in taut narrative realism—by visiting upon them a peculiar, artificial language, allusive, slangy, angular, disillusioned, and searching, uneasily at home in the forms' received constraints and tenets. It's this uneasiness that makes the blending of style and content so potent in film noir, and it's so uneasy because it was so new a thing when it was created. The raw force of creation, of true originality, lasts longer than perhaps any other aesthetic effects. Linguistic invention made it possible for crime fiction and film to dive beneath realism's surfaces, to deepen and make more complex the conventional examination of morality and social anomie their audiences expected, to explore desire, despair, faith, and beauty more richly, more indeterminately and more disturbingly than previously had been possible.

Tennessee, in the years leading up to *Menagerie*, was engaged in a similar quest, trying to adhere to an accurate-enough, familiar-enough representation of reality suitable for narrative realist drama, while attaining, as he specifies in *Menagerie*'s production notes, "a more penetrating and vivid expression of things as they are."

The struggle to find that expression in dramatic form was arduous, filled with second-guessing and self-doubt. On December 11, 1939, for example, he made an entry in his notebook:

> The tragedy of a poet writing drama is that when he writes well—from the dramaturgic, technical point of view he is often writing badly. One must learn—that is the craft, I suppose)—to fuse lyricism and realism into a congruous unit—I guess my chief trouble is that I don't. I make the most fearful faux pas. I feared today that I may have made a distinctly wrong turn in turning to drama—But oh, I do feel drama so intensely some times!

When eventually he succeeded, Tennessee created a new language for the American theater, a new form of stage speech. Arthur Miller recalled in his autobiography, *Timebends*, his reaction upon first encountering this voice:

8

... the words and their liberation, the joy of the writer in writing them, the radiant eloquence of its composition ... unashamed word-joy.... Tennessee had printed a license to speak at full throat.... Language would of course have to be recognizable ... but it seemed possible now to infiltrate it with a kind of superconsciousness ... to lift the experience into emergency speech of an unashamedly open kind rather than to proceed by the crabbed dramatic hints and pretexts of "the natural."

Miller credited hearing the "unashamed word-joy" in *Menagerie* and *A Streetcar Named Desire* as the events that made the writing of *Death of a Salesman* possible.

It was possible for Tennessee to write *The Glass Menagerie* because, by the time he left the shoe factory where his father was frozen in mid-level management, by the time he left St. Louis behind him, abandoning home, Edwina, and his sister Rose, he was already much more the uphill climber toward this immense achievement than the hopeless fugitive, pursued by his two housebound Eumenides, to whom we bid goodbye at the light-extinguishing conclusion of *Menagerie*. Tom flees from the torments of memory, but the playwright was in active pursuit of them, or rather it should be said that he was pursuing the means to embody these tormenting specters onstage. He was also seeking the courage, and maybe the ruthlessness, necessary to do so.

The difficulty of aesthetic discovery no doubt accounted for some of *Menagerie*'s protracted birth. The impulse to write about his family dates back to Tennessee's first dabblings as a writer, and in his letters and notebooks the play emerges and recedes for years before the completed manuscript arrived on Audrey Wood's desk. It competed with other projects, stories, poems, fragments, prototypes of future work, and other plays successfully completed, if not successfully produced, including *Battle of Angels* and *You Touched Me!* He labored on ur-*Menagerie*s, some discarded, some finished, plays about his sister, his mother, and sometimes his father, bearing various titles: *Hawk's Daughter*, *The Spinning Song*, *The Front Porch Girl*, *If You Breathe It Breaks*, *The Pretty Trap*, *Carolers Our Candle*, *A Daughter of the American Revolution*, and, parodying the plays of a competitor, William Saroyan, *Not So Beautiful People* and *The Human Tragedy*.

There were non-writerly distractions, including, once he'd begun in his mid-twenties to have sex with men regularly, an increasingly feverish search for lovers, hustlers, and one-night stands. Occasionally a relationship lasted a short while; he fell deeply in love with a bisexual dancer who broke his heart. There were medical problems, perhaps a mitrovalve prolapse that caused acute panic attacks, and an eye prematurely cataracted almost to complete occlusion. His habit of narcotizing—with alcohol and sleeping pills—his fluttery heart and his anxieties about love, failure, money, family, and madness, was also intensifying. But it's always been too easy to read Tennessee's complicated life as the cautionary tale of a dissolute man squandering his gifts, wresting defeat from the jaws of overwhelming success. If his was a trajectory of dissolution, and in many ways it was, its arc was remarkably long. Tennessee was a strong and determined man and he bore up under what sounds like considerable self-inflicted abuse. Discernible damage to his faculties became evident only after he'd completed three dramatic masterpieces, five or six other plays that are enormously powerful, beautiful, and enduringly stageworthy, as well as a number of superb stories and some lovely poetry. His was neither a speedy nor a conventional dissolution.

And his longest-lasting, grandest compulsion was the act of writing. Neither his substance abuse, which notoriously grew to desperate dimensions, nor his sexual obsession, if that's what it was, nor his wanderlust, his ceaselessly fugitive existence—no other addiction or distraction competed successfully with his habit of writing, daily, every day, till the end of his life. His friends often described him while writing as if in the throes of a trance. More than any other behavior, it was this enviable and alarming superfluent out-pouring of words which continually forced *The Glass Menagerie* off Tennessee's work desk, even as it carried the playwright and his abilities closer and closer to completing it. Writing was both a means of fighting oblivion and of achieving it, of piercing through tranquility and of tranquilizing, simultaneously.

As *Menagerie* began to assume its final form, a process that lasted about four years, it accompanied Tennessee on travels far and wide, through meetings with D. H. Lawrence's widow in New Mexico, through the heartbreak in Provincetown and through a subsequent summer there. The play, or rather its plot, very nearly was sold as the idea for a movie to the man in charge of script development at MGM, and had it sold it likely would never have become a play. The nearly finished manuscript of *Menagerie* was carelessly left behind in the Harvard dorm room of a straight law student when Tennessee abandoned hopes of fucking him ("bed-ding him" or "seducing him" would be more polite but Tennessee would have cackled at these euphemisms). Throughout the final phase of its topsy-turvy, perilous gestation, the play's title was *The Gentleman Caller* (which was the title of the proposed movie as well). This briefly gave way to *The Fiddle in the Wings*, the source of the sentimental music, Tom explains in his opening monologue, which always accompanies memory. Volume One of Tennessee's collected letters suggests that the title likely became *The Glass Me-nagerie* in September 1944.

A menagerie is a Noah's Ark of sorts, in which a variety of spe-cies are collected for the purpose of preservation and exhibition. The inmates of a menagerie are on display, and trapped: a menag-erie is a kind of prison. The translucence and fragility peculiar to the play's eponymous menagerie is illusory: the glass menagerie makes the world outside become transparent, as its images bleed through walls, its dim candlelight penetrates an otherwise engulf-ing darkness. Its bars and walls are far less breakable than those in conventional cells. Tom escapes, but everywhere remains imprisoned.

Menagerie can be said to share more than formal innovation with the crime dramas of film noir. As is frequently the case in noir narration, the monologues in *Menagerie* are spoken by a guilty man who's confessing. The crime Tom confesses is betrayal, which is the central preoccupation of *The Glass Menagerie*. Writing it was an act of betrayal as well. This may help to explain some of the delays, the avoidances, and the difficulties it gave its author on the way to completing it.

While all fiction must incorporate lived experience to be recognizable, to provoke empathy, there's a special anxiety attendant upon the fictionalizing of actual people and events; it grows in intensity the more firmly a work of fiction adheres to the non-fictional. This is partly a result of a fear of the ostensibly insalubrious effects, for audience and artist, of blurring the real and the unreal. Plato and Aristotle worried about the trivializing or subverting of history by presenting it on the stage.

Beyond the communal responsibility to police the boundary between art and life lies the responsibility of the artist to a personal ethics of representation. At the heart of this ethics, concomitant with an understanding of the power of art that's central to the artist's creative impulse, is a fear of transgression through representation—the fear of the graven image, and the fear of art's power over memory, and hence over human history, its violative potential threat to the living and the dead. Shakespeare's Cleopatra wanted to die before she'd be forced to watch herself recreated dramatically, to see "some squeaking Cleopatra boy my greatness/I' th' posture of a whore."

This transgressive anxiety is keener when what's being rendered into fiction is the artist's personal history, his or her autobiography. Consider the pains taken by Eugene O'Neill to hide from public view that other great autobiographical American play, *A Long Day's Journey into Night*, written in 1941, at the same moment that Tennessee was bringing his scattered efforts on *Menagerie* into focus.

O'Neill completed his play three years before Tennessee sent Audrey Wood *Menagerie*. But Tennessee had written *Menagerie*, *Summer and Smoke*, *Streetcar*, *Cat*, *Camino Real*, and *The Rose Tattoo*, and Arthur Miller had written *All My Sons*, *Salesman*, *The Crucible*, and *View From The Bridge*, before either had seen *A Long Day's Journey into Night*, or even knew of its existence. Journey was first staged in Stockholm, in 1956, three years after O'Neill's death. Had his last will and testament been honored, the play wouldn't have been published till 1979. Since its author stipulated in his will that *Journey*, arguably the greatest of all American plays, ought never to be staged, those wishing to disregard O'Neill's intentions would have had to wait till the play entered public domain, in which case (unless Congress extends the length of copyright), *A Long Day's Journey into Night* would still be awaiting its theatrical premiere, which would occur sometime after 2046.

After O'Neill's death, his widow Carlotta, almost certainly lying to a probate court judge, insisted that her husband had locked the play away and interdicted against its stage life because he was worried about the effect its revelation of Ella O'Neill's morphine addiction might have on his son's chances for tenure in the Yale Classics Department. But, she pointed out, since the play's completion and the drafting of the will, Eugene O'Neill Jr. had committed suicide, predeceasing his father. Grief-stricken and gravely ill, according to Carlotta, O'Neill had simply neglected to alter his testamentary instructions for the disposal of the play.

The picture his wife painted of O'Neill placing concerns about his son's career before his own, while not entirely incredible, would have been out of character, to say the least; even if he'd been capable of such paternal sacrifice, it's inconceivable that he would have left the play in Bennett Cerf's vault at Random House because he'd forgotten it was there. Surely, if he had for some reason forgotten it, Carlotta would have reminded him to take it out.

He knew the play was his greatest accomplishment, and after

enough time had passed since the death of his parents and brother, and after his own demise, he wanted it to be read. But staging it was another matter. Following Cleopatra's aversion, O'Neill told Cerf, among others, almost certainly including Carlotta, that he couldn't bear the thought that his parents and brother, and perhaps himself, would be impersonated by actors, squeaking or otherwise, on stage in the naked and flayed condition which *Long Day's Journey* renders them, stripped of all pretenses, their sins and souls laid bare before a theater audience.

O'Neill wrote his four great autobiographical and final dramas in one brief concentrated period between 1939 and 1941, after which he lived for thirteen more years. *The Iceman Cometh*—set in the Fulton Street flophouse in which he attempted suicide in the winter of 1911, before the summer of the events dramatized in *A Long Day's Journey into Night*—was written immediately prior to *Journey*. The foggy summer day and night accounted for in *Journey* preceded O'Neill's admission to the tuberculosis hospital where he began to seriously consider playwriting—a course destined to make him a god in the cosmos in which his penny-pinching father and dangerous brother were merely actors. *Moon for the Misbegotten* and *Hughie* concluded the series, two last attempts to placate, by means of deepening empathic understanding, the perturbed spirit of his brother Jamie.

He'd withdrawn from active participation in the theater, and in public life, to write these plays. In a 1937 paper written at the University of Iowa, Tennessee refers to rumors that O'Neill was dying of tuberculosis. It was a Parkinson's-like neurological affliction, not TB, that was killing him, but the mention made in Tennessee's paper, though inaccurate, is an indication of public awareness that something was happening to the great dramatist, that an end stage had arrived. And indeed it had; after these plays came a decade for O'Neill during which he was capable of very little writing. His increasingly severe tremors made it harder and harder for him to hold a pencil, and the unremitting succession of deaths of family members—father, mother, brother, and son—made his final years a long, virtually uninterrupted period of very private mourning.

O'Neill's post-*Journey* silence is consonant with his desire to hide the play, to banish it from the stage. Even in an age in which publicly exposing oneself and one's family has become an ecstatic and immensely popular entertainment, it's still possible to watch *A Long Day's Journey into Night* and feel, alongside the heartbreak, desolation, horror, and exhilaration into which it reliably propels us, an uneasiness at what the playwright's done to his family. Vast in its forgiveness, *Long Day's Journey* is also an act of unappeasably angry revenge.

O'Neill concluded his career with his autobiographical plays. Tennessee Williams all but began his writing life placing his immediate family onstage, dramatizing the excruciating emancipation necessary for the son to become poet and playwright. In one sense, Tom appears no more emancipated at the end of *Menagerie* than Edmund at the end of *Journey*. Memory, having hounded O'Neill down the years and down the days, arrives as the fearsome household god of the haunted Tyrones; Tennessee's having written the play while young hasn't bought off his ghosts, who intend to hound him wherever he wanders.

If neither play succeeds in putting its author's dead to rest, they nevertheless conclude differently in at least one notable regard: Mary Tyrone speaks, and Amanda Wingfield doesn't. Mary descends among her men like the wraith she's become, trailing her wedding dress—the disquieting disentombing by mothers of their prelapsarian gowns is another gesture shared by *Journey* and *Menagerie*—and her memories silence her husband and sons, struck dumb in the middle of offering a toast. Her voice even causes them to forget their drinks (a big deal in O'Neill's universe: Eugene O'Neill Jr.'s famous suicide note, left by an empty bourbon bottle, read "Never let it be said of O'Neill that he failed to empty a bottle. Ave atque vale."). The Tyrone men cannot recover their tongues, giving Mary the last word. James, Jamie and Edmund fall silent for all sorts of reasons, but memory's power is one of these; Mary's memory transports her, and them, and the play, to the time before any of the three men listening to her had come into her life, before two of them even existed. No wonder they can't drink or speak. Reaching for a remembered happiness, she effectively erases her husband and sons.

This speaking mother/silent son dialectic is reversed at the end of *Menagerie*, when Amanda appears as a voiceless vision, and the concluding speech belongs to Tom, who performs an act of erasure similar to Mary's. Amanda isn't mentioned, and Tom leaves us with the stark, slightly startling fact that it's Laura he's abandoned. It's the loss of Laura that Tom laments, and not only laments. As he ends the play, he's petitioning his sister. She's either acquired or possessed in secret a power, unrevealed in the play until its last sentences: a peculiar power to self-extinguish, and thus set her brother free. It's from Laura that Tom must beg for release.

But Amanda's standing there, Laura's shadow. Tom sees her, and chooses not to address her. The playwright makes us look at her, standing there, unmentioned, which underscores Tom's omission of her name, calls our attention to her banishment from his guilt and grief and to the diminishment of her significance in his heart that this elision implies. It's as unsettling an obliteration as Mary Tyrone's, and we're left with a feeling of deep anger abiding and unresolved, unsettled scores still demanding settlement, of an inextinguishable desire for revenge cohabiting with a mighty but nonetheless vain hope for forgiveness.

In the published version of *Menagerie*, two small surprises precede the text of the play. The first of these is the epigraph, a line from a poem by E. E. Cummings: "Nobody, not even the rain, has such small hands." Who knew that *The Glass Menagerie* had an epigraph? This particular epigraph is mildly surprising because Cummings wasn't a writer Tennessee gave much (or perhaps any other) evidence of admiring, and Tennessee was lavish in his admiration of literary kindred spirits (most of whom were literally spirits: his most cherished writers were dead ones).

The second surprise awaits at the bottom of the original copyright page, in small print: "Copyright 1945 by Tennessee Williams and Edwina D. Williams." Tennessee gave his mother 50% of the royalties from *The Glass Menagerie*. Her share of the revenue generated by her son's enormously successful play gave Edwina a stipend for the rest of her life, and immediately and perhaps more importantly, it enabled her to perform her own version of what her son had already accomplished, or rather what he aspires to, what an inebriated Tom in Scene Four calls "the wonderfullest trick of all, the coffin trick." The magician Tom rather cruelly conjures for his sister (who must know what he means) is a man he's ostensibly seen who was capable of getting out of a coffin without removing any of the nails, an impossible feat Tom fails to emulate, as is witnessed by the play's inconclusive conclusion. Nails have been dislodged, wood's been splintered, the getaway was anything but magical and clean; and worse still, Tom discovers that he hasn't really escaped the coffin, he's merely put wheels on the thing and driven it away.

But he has broken free of the burden of his sister and mother, free of the shoe factory, and soon he'll write a great play. And with half the royalties from that play signed over to her, his mother will manage her own escape from the coffin. Tennessee provided Edwina with financial means sufficient to move out of the house of Cornelius Coffin Williams.

That Tennessee's father took a long time to get around to seeing *The Glass Menagerie*, and had a hard time watching it, is understandable. Edwina Williams's initial public reactions were mainly effusions of maternal pride, accompanied by some nervous disclaimers regarding her resemblance to Amanda Wingfield. One wonders, however, about the ways in which she must have grappled with the paradox with which *Menagerie* confronted her. It realized her grandest ambitions for her adored son, through whose gesture of filial devotion the play's box office would purchase for her freedom from her dreadful husband and secure her a lifelong pension; but this newfound fame and fortune was the consequence of her adored son's exposure, in magnificent stage poetry, of her family's very private agony. And if his love for her was memorialized in *Menagerie's* copyright, the play that follows makes visible for all the world and for all time his anger, perhaps even his hatred of her.

Ella O'Neill had been dead for nearly twenty years before *A Long Day's Journey into Night* was written, and for more than thirty before Mary Tyrone made her first-ever entrance on a stage (speaking in Swedish!). Edwina Williams lived for thirty-five years after the day Laurette Taylor made Amanda Wingfield into an immortal—and for Edwina, an inescapable—figure in world theater. She told anyone who'd listen that she wasn't Amanda, exactly. She wrote (or rather dictated) a book, *Remember Me to Tom*, the forlorn title of which perfectly describes the book's challenge to Tennessee's version of her life, and the baffled estrangement and loss she came to feel about her son.

Gore Vidal, in the course of the same dinner with Tennessee and Edwina mentioned previously, ponders what Tennessee did to his mother by writing the play:

> Currently convinced that the blacks signal to one another during the long St. Louis nights by clanging the lids of the trash cans, Miss Edwina is every inch the Amanda of *The Glass Menagerie*. In fact, so powerful is Tennessee's creation that in the presence of Miss Edwina one does not listen to her but only to what he has made of her.

Though Vidal sounds bemused rather than sympathetic, there's a kind of horror in his description of a real person completely defeated, conquered, subsumed by a fictional one. *Menagerie* was an effective form of revenge.

Tom's and Amanda's moment-to-moment needling of one another is parsed to perfection, their mutual annoyance and exasperation turned into marvelous stage comedy. We recognize how maddening his mother is to Tom, and of greater consequence, what a formidable obstacle she presents to his dream of a meaningful life. But we also see that Tom is in danger of becoming the surly, selfish man his mother accuses him of being, and possibly something worse than that. No one's written better passive-aggressive characters than Tennessee Williams, no one's ever been braver about leaving their manipulative disguises of innocence intact, allowing and requiring productions and audiences to uncover them. In the way Tom quietly, unconsciously packs the keg with gunpowder for an ugly explosion by selecting the already engaged Jim O'Connor as Laura's gentleman caller—an explosion with enough noise and smoke to provide cover for Tom's escape—he must be considered almost the equal of that undisputed champion of passive aggression, Stella DuBois.

The playwright's admiration and affection for the woman on whom he based Amanda Wingfield, or at least for the dramatic character he made of that woman, is evident not only in his lifelong connection to Edwina, but in the way he wrote her counterpart. In the "provisional film story treatment" for *The Gentleman Caller*, the movie *Menagerie* might have become had MGM not rejected it, Tennessee describes Amanda as "a conventional woman, a little foolish and pathetic, but with an heroic fighting spirit concentrated blindly on trying to create a conventionally successful adjustment for two children who are totally unfitted for it." He goes further: "Amanda represents the natural elegance in the Old South. My main theme is a defense of the romantic attitude towards life, a violent protest against the things that destroy it. Amanda represents that." By the time this film treatment became *The Glass Menagerie*, Amanda had become less a foreshadow of Blanche DuBois; certainly for Tom, she's as destructive of "the romantic attitude towards life" as she is its last refuge and incarnation. But her opposition to Tom's dreamy unfitness is grounded in reason, not barbarism or malice, and if in *Menagerie* Amanda is less "conventional" than the character he described to MGM's Story Department, she remains arguably just as heroic. This leaves us to wonder about the source of the angry, unforgiving aftertaste the play leaves regarding her, and about Tennessee's intentions in making, at the outset of his career, a public spectacle, however magnificent, of the private pain of living people.

Tom resents the way that Amanda, a tough and practical-minded adversary, forces him back, over and over again, to consideration of the plight of his sister, her helplessness and his responsibility to help her survive in a world for which she's unsuited. In the MGM treatment, both brother and sister are "unfitted" for the world; similarly, in a journal entry describing the plot of the never-written *Hawk's Daughter*, we hear of a brother and sister who are "sensitive, terrified children." But by the time Tennessee's inchoate autobiographical impulses had coalesced in *The Glass Menagerie*, there's no parity between brother and sister in terms of disability. Tom may be doomed to feel guilty forever, but he's not doomed. He'll escape the coffin; a messy escape is better than none at all. Laura's life after Tom's departure is too terrible to contemplate.

This is a good moment to return to the short story, "Portrait of a Girl in Glass," the central character of which is Laura, who remains the center of the story when it becomes *Menagerie*'s plot. Though Amanda surges forward forcefully to dominate the play, and though Laura is a role of such reticence and silence that it's all too easy for an actress to underwhelm, we're made acutely aware by the end that Laura is, has always been, the narrator/author's principal, and maybe his only, concern.

Laura is Tennessee's sister Rose, two years older than he. After a troubled early adolescence, Rose was sent to a Missouri state psychiatric hospital, Farmington, in 1937. Diagnosed as "Dementia Precox (Schizophrenic) Mixed Type, Paranoid Predominating," Rose remained in Farmington till Tennessee had the means to move her to a private sanitarium in Connecticut in 1949, and then to another sanitarium in Ossining, New York, where she lived till her death at the age of eighty-six.

On January 13, 1943, a few months before Tennessee wrote "Portrait of a Girl in Glass," shortly before commencing in earnest his work on *The Glass Menagerie*, Rose went into surgery for a bilateral frontal lobotomy.

Her six years in Farmington prior to the lobotomy had been a gruesome siege, involving the use of insulin and Metrazol for a regimen of chemically induced convulsive shock therapy, which quieted Rose temporarily but never for long. Edwina and her mother, Tennessee's revered grandmother Dakin, were Rose's only regular visitors. Tennessee found visiting his sister unbearable, while Cornelius seems to have decided that Rose no longer existed, refusing not only to visit her but to have any role in her treatment.

This left Edwina alone to decide whether or not Rose would be lobotomized. Rose's doctors assured Edwina that the surgery had been successful in cases similar to that of her otherwise untreatable daughter, and Edwina consented. The lobotomy was done, and it seems to have made Rose more docile, easier to handle, though not sane.

Before and after the surgery, Edwina tormented herself about giving her consent. It's difficult not to see the decision as punitive and violent. Tennessee seems to have felt that it was. After the lobotomy was done, he wrote in his notebook:

A cord breaking.
1000 miles away.
Rose. Her head cut open.
A knife thrust in her brain.
Me. Here. Smoking.
My father, mean as a devil, snoring. 1000 miles away.

Tennessee was in Manhattan at the time of the surgery. In the entry, he confronts the essentially violent, violating nature of the procedure, making it sound like a rape. Apart from Rose, Tennessee mentions himself, far away and smoking—which makes him both a distant figure, taking pleasure at ease or at worst brooding comfortably, and also something that's burning up. There's nothing ambiguous about his feelings toward his father. There is ambiguity, however, in the final "1000 miles away." Cornelius was in St. Louis at the time, about seventy miles away. "1000 miles away" might refer to the emotional distance this unconscious snoring pig has placed between himself and his daughter. And it might be meant to refer to Tennessee's distance, not only from his sister in her moment of peril, but from his Devil of a father; in other words, the price of his freedom from Cornelius is his abandonment of Rose.

Edwina isn't mentioned. It took thirteen years for her stage persona to transmogrify from Amanda Wingfield to the fiendish Violet Venable, the mother in *Suddenly Last Summer* who seeks to have her niece lobotomized in order to extirpate certain truths from her brain. *Suddenly Last Summer* was written in 1957, the same year in which Cornelius died, and Tennessee began working with a psychoanalyst who among other things encouraged him to forgive his father and to acknowledge repressed rage at his mother. And perhaps he was encouraged as well to displace onto her some of the guilt he'd been carrying around.

The most intolerable aspect of Rose's madness for the Williamses, including Tennessee, seems to have been her sexual acting-out. Even her doctors express dismay about it in their reports. She'd begun to dress inappropriately before she was institutionalized, and to produce an unstoppable stream of dirty talk about masturbation, sexual longing, her own body, and Tennessee's. After visiting Rose in Farmington in December of 1939—so disturbing to him that it would be his last visit before the lobotomy—he wrote in his notebook:

> Visited Rose at sanitarium—horrible, horrible! Her talk was so obscene—she laughed and spoke continual obscenities ...

The entry goes on, Tennessee's grief at his sister's insanity becoming tinged with something like hysteria:

... Everything seems useless and ugly now—hideously smirched—After all her naked subconscious is no uglier than the concealed thoughts of others—And is sex ugly? Not essentially—not from a cosmic viewpoint. But when it is divorced from reason—it looks like slime—it seems horrible you can't reason it away. Poor mad creature—if only it didn't make you so hideous you wouldn't dread it so much—

To this final peculiar notion, he appended a knowing parenthetical question: "(To whom is this last line addressed?)"

Well might he ask. The young Thomas Lanier Williams was very close to his older sister, and when she began to lose her mind he became terrified that he would lose his as well. This terror never left him. That Rose's insanity took the form of an unembarrassed, hyperactive carnality must have intensified her closeted gay brother's identification, as well as his dread. Rose, before her lobotomy, was speaking aloud about desires that Tennessee wasn't ready to articulate above a very discreet whisper.

A clue to the existence, in Tennessee's mind, of an equation of his and Rose's illegitimate appetites can be found in the word "disgust," which Tennessee repeatedly used to describe Rose's sexual conduct. In a vicious letter he wrote to Rose when both were in their mid-twenties, regarding the news he'd received that she'd come on to a boy, "I want you to know that you disgusted me." In a journal entry from 1936, he records that Rose "trails around in negligees," and then adds: "Disgusting." In 1939, he added to this entry a marginal note: "God forgive me for this."

The word "disgust" occupies a famous moment in his greatest play, in which a woman hisses it into the ear of her young husband, whom she's just discovered having sex with another man: "I know. I saw. You disgust me." The loathing, hatred, rejection packed into the word leads directly to her husband's suicide. Blanche never asks God to forgive her, and is absolutely unable ever to forgive herself.

The Glass Menagerie has an almost genteel tone, different from any of Tennessee's subsequent plays—indeed it's rather different than much of the writing that precedes it. Levrich's biography quotes from a *Time* magazine article about Tennessee entitled "The Winner," written after Menagerie's New York opening. The newly famous playwright warns the reporter, and his audience,

> In this play I have said all the nice things I have to say about people. The future things will be much harsher.

A few months later he told the reporter for *The Portland Oregonian*, for an article called "Bang Bang Plays Disgust, Fascinate *Glass* Author,"

> *The Glass Menagerie* has for me the peculiar importance of being the first play that I have managed to write without succumbing to the undeniable fascination of violence. It is my first quiet play, and perhaps my last.

It sounds as though Tennessee felt a cautiously expressed, minor dissatisfaction with *Menagerie*, some reticence in it he intended, immediately, to overcome. His next works treat their characters more roughly, and the characters treat one another more roughly; but the most noticeable difference between his first acclaimed play and those that follow is that *The Glass Menagerie* is among the least sexual texts in any medium that Tennessee Williams ever wrote.

Tom is undoubtedly seething with repressed or suppressed desires, but he never discusses these with his mother, his sister or with the audience. There's a yearning for elsewhere in his monologues, and the beauty of his language is erotic; there's yearning in the void his sullen silences create while Amanda chatters about jonquils on Blue Mountain. But apart from a couple of thin hints of a sexual life either dreamed of or attempted, Tom is guarded and demure. There's a southern randiness, beguiling and heartbreaking, in Amanda's obsessive recollection of the dating rituals of her youth, but this, too, is demure.

Laura's neurasthenia and shyness are so depressingly engulfing that the play's revelation of her, in Scene Seven—the play's greatest scene—as a young woman with a hidden but active sexual fantasy life, seems a miraculous transformation, impossible to watch without hoping for more miracles, for something impossible: that the play will turn out differently this time, that Jim will fall in love with her, make her happy, save her.

The previously mentioned final difference between "Portrait of a Girl in Glass" and *The Glass Menagerie* has to do with Laura, who in the short story is not physically disabled and doesn't wear a leg brace, nor is she sickly. If she'd had pleurosis as a girl, it isn't mentioned. The narrator of "Portrait" says his sister is unclassifiable, but he describes her in the grip of an acute, paralyzing agoraphobia: "She made no positive motion towards the world but stood at the edge of the water, so to speak, with feet that anticipated too much cold to move."

Laura resembles her namesake character in *Menagerie* in terms of paralysis. In the short story Laura's a little livelier, an impression mainly derived from Tennessee having given her a romantic disposition in place before Jim's arrival, which feels at least adolescent, more sexually mature than the prepubescent, childlike fantasies of *Menagerie*'s Laura. The old records that Laura listens to in the short story, having belonged to her runaway father, have a pedigree of loss and love, with juicy titles like "The Love Nest," "Whispering," and "I Love You." Laura in "Portrait" doesn't merely listen to these records, she sings along.

She reads as well, an activity which Laura in *Menagerie* has either never done or doesn't mention. In "Portrait," Laura has two novels, one of which she doesn't read and one which she reads repeatedly. The latter is *Freckles*, by the female romance novelist Gene Stratton-Porter (a name that would have been familiar to readers in the 1940s). Laura's clearly in love with the novel's Horatio Alger–type protagonist, a one-armed boy named Freckles, who's in love with a girl he calls the Swamp Angel, of whom Laura feels jealous. By a sheer coincidence that may nevertheless encourage Laura to see him as her destiny, "Freckles" turns out to be the nickname of her gentleman caller, Jim.

These meager but spicy details make Laura's life in "Portrait" a little less barren than it seems in *Menagerie*. They give Laura less asphyxiatingly limited appetites and activities than the ones she gives the impression of possessing in the play when, asked by Jim to talk about her interests, she can only talk about her glass animal collection. In a brilliant dramatic gesture, Tennessee leads us to feel mortified by Laura's weirdly impoverished, nutty world when she decides to share it with Jim; then we're made to feel ashamed of our ungenerous response when Jim, rather than being alarmed, dismayed, or repulsed, is moved by her trust, charmed by her fragility, even seduced by her fantasies.

But no matter how delightful her otherness may be to Jim, the play's resourceless Laura—her happiness, her future, perhaps her sanity—depends to a frightening degree on the kindness of, in this case, a single stranger. The girl in "Portrait," while developmentally arrested, is slightly less destitute of possibilities, and her life after Tom leaves is a more open question.

In "Portrait," Tennessee gives Laura a line, spoken after the departure of her gentleman caller, which he chose to take away from Laura in the play. Once Jim has gone:

> Laura was the first to speak.
> "Wasn't he nice?" she asked. "And all those freckles!"
> "Yes," said Mother. Then she turned to me.
> "You didn't mention that he was engaged to be married!"
> "Well how did I know that he was engaged to be married?"
> "I thought you called him your best friend down at the warehouse?"
> "Yes, but I didn't know he was going to be married!"
> "How peculiar!" said Mother. "How very peculiar!"

Thus far, the dialogue in this scene of "Portrait" is very close to the lines in the play. But now the two diverge. After this point in the play, Amanda and Tom keep at one another till Tom leaves, propelled by his mother's glorious, terrible curse: "Go to the moon, you selfish dreamer!"

Laura, from whom nothing more is heard in *Menagerie* after Jim leaves, in the short story has something to say:

> "How peculiar!" said Mother. "How very peculiar!"
> "No," said Laura gently, getting up from the sofa. "There's nothing peculiar about it."
> She picked up one of the records and blew on its surface, as if it were dusty, then set it softly back down.
> "People in love," she said, "take everything for granted."
> What did she mean by that? I never knew.
> She slipped quietly back into her room and closed the door.

What *does* Laura mean by that? It's fairly obvious that she means that Tom is in love. Tom is in love with Jim, and, because he desires it to be so, he's taken it for granted that Jim isn't the kind to get engaged. We can read Tom's failure to understand Laura as a willed obtuseness, abetted by the shock of being unceremoniously outed, by his mousey sister, with his mother present.

Or perhaps the person Laura believes Tom to be in love with is not Jim, but Laura herself. She could be implying that Tom takes for granted her indifference regarding Jim's availability, because he assumes she reciprocates her brother's feelings for him.

While nothing suggests that Tennessee had an incestuous relationship with his sister, his love for her, and, he felt (despite her ruined mind) hers for him, lasted his lifetime, and beyond: he gave Edwina half the royalties to *Menagerie*, but he left his entire estate, in trust, to Rose. She was, in many ways, the one constant in his life, its enduring emotional center. The editor of his journals, Margaret Bradham Thornton, lists more than fifteen completed plays and fragments by Tennessee in which a character based on Rose appears, more than eight poems he wrote about her, a dozen plays in which mental illness and lobotomies feature prominently, and over ten plays and fragments in which Rose's name is used.

Their connection was tempered in childhood, when they were mutually victimized by their father. Rose got the worst of it. Cornelius was openly emotionally abusive to his daughter; this worsened as she reached puberty, and, on the basis of Rose's increasing hatred for him—so intense that at one point, before she was sent to Farmington, her doctors warned Edwina that Cornelius's life was at risk—there's been speculation that Rose may have been sexually as well as emotionally abused by Cornelius.

Tennessee's love for Rose was of a piece with his guilt over their unequal fortunes, and his abiding, frightened conviction that he shared with her at least the potential for mental illness, manifest differently in each—his terrible anxiety attacks and insomnia, her psychosis—and manifest in one similar way, namely their socially unacceptable, untamable sexualities.

In "Portrait of a Girl in Glass," Tennessee permitted Rose's surrogate to bring love, and with it sexual desire, into the little flat in East St. Louis, and to cause its carnal flush to spread over Tom, threatening to reveal his homosexuality, and perhaps even to cast their loving sibling relationship in indecent colors. She does this in a line that's decorous and raw, sentimental and rudely aggressive. Inasmuch as she calls Tom out for what he's done, and pays him back for his carelessness, or his cruelty, with cruelty of her own, the short-story version of Laura is formidable. Having struck back at her brother, having exposed the sexual longings beneath her brother's dreaminess, she goes to her room, closing the door behind her. She shuts Tom out. She leaves first.

The two paragraphs that follow the passage quoted above, which conclude "Portrait of a Girl in Glass," are nearly identical to Tom's final monologue in *Menagerie*. But in "Portrait" there's no final prayer to Laura's ghost for forgiveness or forgetting. Instead,

> ... A door comes softly and irresistibly open. I hear the tired old music my unknown father left in the place he abandoned as faithlessly as I. I see the faint and sorrowful radiance of the glass, hundreds of little transparent pieces of it in very delicate colors. I hold my breath, for if my sister's face appears among them—the night is hers!

At the end of "Portrait," Laura does not merely haunt, she possesses! Like most people, she becomes dangerous when she's injured—Laura in "Portrait of a Girl in Glass," that is, but not in *The Glass Menagerie*.

In *Menagerie*, Laura doesn't have a room to go into or a door to close behind her; she sleeps in the living room. When Jim leaves, covering sheepishness and regret with "a cheery shout," Laura in the play may do anything an actress and director want, but in the text, Tennessee deposited her in a crouch by the Victrola, winding it, withdrawn as Jim leaves, and for the remainder of the scene, as Tom and Amanda fight, the playwright seems to have forgotten Laura, who's given neither lines nor stage direction, only reappearing in Tom's last memory.

More than Tom's chief concern, Laura in "Portrait" is the principle source of his grief and guilt; more than a tormenting memory, she's his nemesis, his chief adversary.

Much the same can be said of Laura in *Menagerie*, but it's left unsaid, by Laura, by Tom, and by the playwright.

One further possible interpretation of what Laura meant, at the end of "Portrait," in her response to Tom: the "everything" Laura accuses Tom of taking for granted isn't Jim's homosexuality, but her fidelity to Tom, her passive devotion to her brother, her willingness to be used as a pretext for Tom to bring a man he desires closer to him, regardless of how unsuitable that engaged-to-be-married man is for Laura, or for that matter, how unsuitable this heterosexual man is for Tom. Perhaps Laura is accusing Tom of pursuing his sexual longing with heartless solipsism.

In this, Laura's accusation in "Portrait" may be considered as a first iteration of the truth that, in *Suddenly Last Summer*, Mrs. Venable wants to slice out of her niece Catherine Holly's brain: Catherine's memory contains certain knowledge that Mrs. Venable's murdered poet son, Sebastian, was gay. Catherine knows because Sebastian used her as bait to attract the boys he wanted to fuck (who eventually tear him to pieces).

When he wrote *Suddenly Last Summer*, Tennessee made semi-public his conviction that Edwina had agreed to have Rose loboto-mized not to cure her but to strip her memory and her speech of its embarrassing, garish sexual content, speech from which Edwina sought to shield the ears of her sons (Tennessee and his younger brother, Dakin) and her husband, speech which Tennessee, hearing his sexual self implicated and exposed, found unbearable.

"*After a while*"—he wrote in the stage direction that precedes the wonderfully reluctant, indeterminate last line of *Suddenly Last Summer*, spoken by the maddeningly ineffectual Doctor Sugar: "I think we ought to at least consider the possibility that the girl's story could be true …"—Tennessee was emotionally ready, and professionally secure enough, to go rather far, for the time, in risk-ing self-exposure as a sexually active gay man. Indeed, by 1957, ho-mosexuality had been featured prominently in several of his plays, beginning with *Streetcar*. By the late 1950s, Tennessee was more nearly out of the closet than most other mainstream artists (Gore Vidal would be an exception), more than almost all American ho-mosexuals of the period felt they could afford to be.

Thirteen years earlier, however, trying to win the acclaim, for-tune, and most importantly for him, the audience he knew he had the talent to win and to hold, Tennessee was writing considerably more carefully. Even the gossamer sexuality he explores in "Por-trait of a Girl in Glass," for which he had no immediate publication plans, is more or less entirely expunged from *The Glass Menagerie*. All that's left of sex in the play is what we can infer might take place during Tom's nocturnal absences. That these are anathema to Amanda could be proof that we're inferring correctly, though she may fear Tom's lust less than his wanderlust. If he was getting laid, he might not want to leave St. Louis so badly.

Hence Laura in *Menagerie*. "She should be lit like a saint or a Madonna," the playwright commands future lighting designers in the production notes that preface the script. Along with slides featuring "a swarm of typewriters" or lines of French poetry ("ou sont les neiges"), lighting designers may disregard Tennessee's questionable taste when it comes to lighting Laura, but there's nothing that the character says or does, except in the aforementioned scene alone with Jim, and even there not very much, that would feel dissonant with an electrically supplied virginal numen.

As she is transposed from unpublished short story to produced play, Laura loses—along with much of her sexuality—autonomy, agency, and a very good line of dialogue. It's arguable whether *The Glass Menagerie* would be improved had that line been imported from "Portrait," along with other manifestations of the richer, stronger inner life and resilience its version of Laura possesses. The play's so close to being a perfect realization of its ambitions that it's almost unthinkable to criticize any aspect of it; it would be beyond foolish to second-guess a very great artist at the commencement of a period of sublime accomplishment. Laura presenting the audience with a moment of powerful ambiguity immediately before the curtain descends might well have been, in a play so elegantly elegiac, a dreadful dramaturgical misstep that Tennessee chose wisely to avoid, and in any event *Menagerie* is too central, too loved and familiar, inevitable and unalterable, to be able to countenance any road not taken as an opportunity lost.

Nevertheless, in *The Glass Menagerie* Tennessee resurrected his sister Rose, and at the same time circumscribed her. He spent the early years of his writing life grappling with how to approach his sister's tragedy without drowning in its oceanic, ongoing sorrow; he also had to find a way to bring his empathic gifts, his power as a writer, to bear on a subject that threatened, through identification, through his sense of his and Rose's shared pathology and destiny, to disempower and disable him.

At some moment in 1942, before "Portrait" or the final phase of work on *Menagerie*, Tennessee wrote a verse play, *The Purification*, about an incestuous relationship between a brother and sister. After the sister, Rosalia, has been murdered by her husband, the brother/narrator apostrophizes her: "For nothing contains you now, no, nothing contains you, lost little girl, my sister." There is terrible loss in this cry, and also a kind of awestruck terror, as if Rosalia is, in death, released from a prison and in her freedom she becomes uncontainable, unbounded.

There's torment in containment, and also safety, at least for the jailer, and possibly for the jailed. Menageries, and closets, contain.

The man who created some of the greatest roles for women in American drama was able to do so because he deeply identified with the female characters who populate his plays: their emotional and imaginative capacities, their desires, and their unfitness, abjection and doom. As deeply as he identified, he also feared these women, battled and ran from them. For Tennessee they possess a ghostly power, some overwhelming force that flows through them from which he fled, and from which male surrogates in the plays, beginning with Tom, unsuccessfully attempt to flee. The great overarching project of Tennessee's best plays, if such a thing can be legitimately described, is his struggle over the mysterious nature of this power that belongs to the abject and powerless.

The E. E. Cummings line that Tennessee found for *Menagerie's* epigraph is a curious choice for the play. "Nobody, not even the rain, has such small hands," which must refer to Laura—to whom else in the play could it possibly refer?—is taken from a poem, "somewhere i have never traveled, gladly beyond," addressed to a woman by her lover.

The evocation of the rain casts a melancholic spell of gloomy skies, of dissolving and tears appropriate enough for *Menagerie*. And perhaps Tennessee was drawn to the poem when seeking an epigraph for this play about his lost sister because its penultimate line is "the voice of your eyes is deeper than all roses."

Melancholy it may be, but the epigraph sounds like a whispered diminutive endearment, consonant with the poem of erotic intimacy of which it's the concluding line.

The diminutive regresses the beloved, as diminutives do; the smallest hands belong to children. And so, as happens when lovers use diminutives, the erotic and the parental/familial are elided. We seek to regress our lovers not only because we harbor repressed incestuous desires, but because we thus erotically invest the responsibility for the other we take on when we fall in love and make love. We're in bed with a lover, who's turning us on and fucking us; who is at the same time a beloved, a burden we've erotically cathected and come to desire.

Earlier in the poem, Cummings writes:

nothing which we are to perceive in this world equals
the power of your intense fragility

The rain's small hands have power, of course. One thinks of the ineluctable action of water, seeking out the narrowest crevices and cracks, widening them, slipping past all barriers, eroding what's solid through slow attrition.

But this power is little represented in *The Glass Menagerie*. If Cummings intends for us to consider how our lovers may possess the attritional powers of the rain to transform, to destroy, Tennessee follows the epigraph with a play from the center of which, in the character of Laura, active power, even small-handed active power, is as absent as the absconded Wingfield patriarch. What's present in *Menagerie* is the power of intense fragility, a power dependent on kindness, on the desire of another to protect the frail thing and prevent its breaking, a passive power that works through love.

Tennessee's intention, avowed in his notebooks, his letters and essays, and manifest in his plays, stories and poems, was to bring the power of intense fragility center stage in the American theater, to give it representation, to parse its essence and proclaim it as an essential component energy in the dynamics of human life. He also gave representation to the adversary of fragility, to the aggressive,

33

steamrolling, bullying violence so familiar to him from life with his father, and which alone was recognizable to his country and his historical period as power and strength. He knew himself and the fugitive kind for whom he felt appointed to speak to be at odds with, even locked in battle against, implacable forces of history ascending, as he labored on *Menagerie*, to an apotheosis of savagery and barbarism. His championing of the power of intense fragility was as radical as his faith in the power of that intensely fragile thing, art. Frailty and art were, for Tennessee, intrinsic to one another. He was an aesthete, of sorts.

"The artist is made out of an especially perishable substance," Tennessee wrote in "Comments on the Nature of Artists with a few Specific References to the Case of Edgar Allen Poe," the 1937 college paper, written while a student at the University of Iowa, in which he reported premature rumors of O'Neill's imminent death:

> ... this is a fact which literary biography leaves beyond dispute. This may suggest that art is a compensatory gesture: something that the owner takes up to compensate for physiological or nervous weakness just as a blind person may develop acute auditory and tactile senses. I think it is rather a demonstration of the tremendous drain that the creative energy makes upon the physical being. Artists have always been prone to degenerative diseases like tuberculosis: the greatest of the moderns were afflicted with respiratory disorders: Chekhov, Mansfield died of tuberculosis: Marcel Proust of a similar disease: O'Neill has an arrested case of tuberculosis. It is rumored that he is now dying of it. Sidney Lanier [Tennessee's ancestor] struggled against that disease his whole creative life. John Keats died of it. Nervous maladies are so general among artists as to be almost universal. To offer a list of nervously afflicted artists would be an extravagant use of paper.

His abandonment for the purposes of paper conservation of this catalogue of "nervously afflicted artists" raises the suspicion that Tennessee was not entirely confident about his thesis; he later dismissed the paper as "silly." At the University of Iowa he was still dating women; he may have realized he was revealing too much about his "extravagant" and "silly" self.

Or he may have disowned the paper, with its totem list of neurasthenic artists, because of an inability to comfortably straddle one of aestheticism's central contradictions. The conflation of art and fragility—whether through ephemerality, infirmity or some other source of weakness—obscures another truth about art, specifically that exuberance, toughness, aggression, and perhaps competitiveness and ruthlessness as well are requisite character traits in artists. Tennessee acknowledges this when, in the paper, he proposes that the ill-health artists are prone to may not be the precondition as much as it is the consequence of being artists. The "tremendous drain the creative process makes upon the physical being" would surely crush physical beings who aren't reasonably healthy to begin with.

In a journal entry on December 4, 1941, in the throes of the kind of despair all working writers are prone to, Tennessee prayed to three of his literary divinities, Walt Whitman, Anton Chekhov, and Hart Crane, for sustenance and courage. He set them in a hierarchy, because, out of the depths, he besought vigor, not fragility:

> Old Walt—Look out for me, will you? It's no use asking Hart Crane or Chekhov—They were too sick themselves.

Whitman embodied, in his writing and in his actual body, which he repeatedly described, a robust muscularity, authority and indefatigable expansiveness. Tennessee casts him in a similar role, again in the company of Chekhov and Crane, in the poem "Sailor's Memoranda":

> My personal trinity let me think of them,
> Whitman the brawler, the cosmic-voyager Crane,
> And soft-spoken Chekhov on evenings of wind and rain.

Although Whitman famously called himself "one of the roughs," he wasn't much of a "brawler," which makes him sound less like a rough and more like rough trade. Whitman's genius combined force and gentleness, giddily priapic and tenderly nurturing or sorrow-ing—in this his work resembles that of D. H. Lawrence, another writer of ceaseless, surging, even phallic potency whom Tennessee idolized (though by the period of the writing of *Menagerie* Lawrence seems to have been eclipsed by the trinity cited above). Whitman steps in and out of roles, including gender, with the universally in-clusive, infinitely generous narcissism that's his own special brand of empathy. Real brawlers were only tricks for Tennessee, a scary night's amusement, never keepers. He cherished Whitman because he was a rough (or posed as one, but that's another story) who was cognizant of the intense power of fragility, who understood, as he wrote in the preface to the first edition of *Leaves of Grass*, that "the indirect is always as great and real as the direct."

"Soft-spoken" Chekhov, initially dismissed in the December 4 journal entry as too likely consumed with his own debilities to come to the aid of the frustrated writer, is given an immediate second glance and a reconsideration. "Well, maybe Chekhov," Ten-nessee decides in the entry's next sentence. "He'd be tender. But Crane—Heaven what nonsense!"

In Tennessee's trinity, manifestations of conventionally defined power rank above intense fragility, are valued more than inward-ness and powerlessness. And thus is the purely visionary Crane grumpily demoted from "cosmic-voyager" with "Heaven what nonsense!" Non-visionary, non-heavenly, profoundly human Chekhov is provisionally redeemed because, in his stories and plays, he manifests tenderness. His writing is outer- rather than inner-directed; its miraculous empathy makes it capable of provid-ing shelter, as Tennessee saw it, against wind and rain. Though one of the frail ones—not a brawler—he has power, he can be of use.

The Russian dramatist was key, in fact, for the young American trying to find a way to give forceful representation to the ineffable, to limn with strong, confident strokes the nearly invisible.

"I'm raving," Tennessee unhappily continues in the December 4 entry, though what follows is less delusional than self-pitying:

> Why can't I write like Chekhov?
> I could gouge my good eye out because I can't do something lovely and haunting like "The Sea Gull".
> Yes—raving.

Tennessee wrote a paper while attending Washington University in St. Louis in the spring of 1937, entitled "Birth of an Art (Anton Chekhov and the New Theater)." It's rather a bold title for an undergraduate, and rather a thrilling one, given who that undergraduate was to become. He calls *The Seagull* "a tragedy of inaction."

> The essential idea behind this play is the aimless frustration of certain lives ...
> What happens to them is mainly outside of their control. Circumstances make them captive ... a tangle in which all are helpless victims; no one is really to blame.

Tennessee located and delighted in Chekhov's still-shocking suspension of the overt, melodramatic moralizing of most nineteenth-century drama, the departure from which is a great part of what made Chekhov's plays revolutionary—so revolutionary, in fact, that a number of people, including Leo Tolstoy, couldn't comprehend them or even recognize them as plays. But his collegiate account of *The Seagull* doesn't do justice to the vast complexity of Chekhov's moral universe or to *The Seagull*, which has its share of victims but also of blameworthy characters, arguably more blameworthy than any other characters in Chekhov's great plays.

A "tragedy of inaction" seems as if it ought to address the consequences for people when they fail to act, which is neither what happens in *The Seagull* nor what Tennessee contends is happening. The play he describes might more properly be called a tragedy of futility—except that's an oxymoron, inasmuch as will, choice, and action are inherent in, if not definitive of, all conceptions of tragedy. His professor, Otto Heller, wasn't buying any of it: he returned the paper with the comment that it "in no way fulfills the require-ments of a term paper as indicated repeatedly. All of this, or nearly all, was written without reference or relation to literary standards and criteria as studied in the course." Fair enough, since the paper includes the sentence "I will not attempt to give the names of the Russian characters as they are both difficult to spell and pronounce and I have returned the plays to the library …"

Tennessee read and analyzed to satisfy requirements of his own, finding in his version of Chekhov the kind of plays he was strug-gling to create. "The charm of [*The Seagull*]," he wrote,

> is in its haunting atmosphere and the emotional poignance built by each scene. It has an exquisite unity of color: a sort of nostalgic twilight pervades it from the beginning.

The Seagull's bucolic, summertime setting is fantastically at odds with the demonic passions wreaking havoc among its company of arriviste artists and artists manqué. Their passionate cruelty, envy, pettiness, rapacity and their abject terror—of failure, abandonment, poverty and mortality—result in their bloody ruination; their every action to fend off what they fear brings their every terror closer, espe-cially death, which at the end comes home to roost in this pastoral hell.

Surely Tennessee was aware of the brutal carryings-on in Arka-dina's charnel/summer house. He was far too sensitive a reader not to have noticed that the atmosphere in *The Seagull* is toxic, and if it has a unified color, that color is close to black. The twilit, nostalgic atmosphere he praises in *The Seagull* is much more recognizably that of the comparatively gentle memory play he would eventually write. A "tangle" of hopeless helplessness is less an apt description of the carnal, exploitive, bloody world of *The Seagull* than an antici-pation of the closed-coffin claustrophobia of *The Glass Menagerie*.

When he wrote that he found charm at work in *The Seagull*, Tennessee likely intended the older, more solemn meaning of that word: the power to cast a spell, to bewitch, to alter and transform reality by potent magic. The aspect of Chekhov's dramaturgy that spoke to him most persuasively was its apparent suspension of rules of grand action and, until the gruesome conclusion, violent conflict. He was taken with the way an almost motionless, almost frozen, almost anti-dramatic representation of life can, in its powerful fragility, contain and express tragedy's enormous power.

The most direct evidence of Chekhov's influence on Tennessee's breakthrough play isn't from Chekhov's breakthrough *Seagull* but rather from the last of his four dramatic masterpieces, *The Cherry Orchard*. Among those who'd had their theatrical horizons significantly widened by seeing Alla Nazimova play *Orchard*'s Ranevskaya were Eugene O'Neill, in New York, and Tennessee, when Nazimova's tour arrived in St. Louis. In the spring of 1944, as Tennessee was finishing *Menagerie*, Eva Le Gallienne left the role of Ranevskaya in a celebrated, long-running Broadway version of *The Cherry Orchard*; she was replaced by Margaret Webster, whose previous gig had been as director of Tennessee's *Battle of Angels*, his first professional production and a notorious flop.

The private conversation between Laura and Jim in Scene Seven in *The Glass Menagerie*, the all-too-brief instant in which Laura steps out of the shadows and claims, in her tentative way, as much of center stage, and as much of joy and romantic love as she'll ever be offered, is, as has previously been stated, the heart of the play. It's the moment in which everything beautiful, wrenching, funny and frightening in the scenes that precede it gather together and plunge two of the play's characters (and not the two we'd been expecting) into a place of impossible possibility, of hope as necessary as it is implausible, an infinitely vulnerable place the decimation of which is nearly unbearable. It's the dramatic moment which announced that a great playwright had discovered his voice, that something new in dramatic literature had arrived, and consequently, something more could be expected from theater.

Without taking anything away from its originality, an inspiration and model for this scene is to be found in *The Cherry Orchard*, in the very short dialogue (twelve lines!) in which the orchard's new owner, Lopakhin, comes close to rescuing Varya, who adores him, from a future of loneliness and servitude, and doesn't; in this he fails to rescue himself as well. Chekhov found the scene nearly impossible to write. His first attempt ended with Lopakhin proposing to Varya; Chekhov then abandoned work on the play for two days and, after anaesthetizing himself by getting drunk, tore up Lopakhin's and Varya's happiness and wrote what is one of his greatest and most devastating scenes, the culmination of his genius for describing dramatically how the world can come to an end during a desultory conversation about galoshes, the weather and a broken thermometer.

Like Lopakhin, Jim is representative of a formerly servile class now in triumphant ascendance over an impaupered, befuddled, dying aristocracy. Jim's modernity, expressed in his confidence-building self-improvement monologues, moves, scares and emboldens Laura, who shyly begins to welcome him as a fresh breeze able to blow away the cobwebs in which she's suffocating. Varya has found similar thrills of virility, vitality, and futurity in the just barely modern business-oriented brazenness of semi-barbaric Lopakhin.

The scene between Jim and Laura in *Menagerie* is several times the length of its *Orchard* antecedent, but this is in part because Tennessee had to provide time on stage for Laura to fall in love, and for Jim to detect in her strangeness the human soul of which his self-improvement courses are demanding he divest himself; only then is the stage set for the tragic near-miss to occur.

Jim's already engaged, and is far less likely than Lopakhin to propose marriage; but we feel that he's lost as important a chance, at the end of the scene with Laura, as Laura has, and he's the more culpable, because agency resides more comfortably in him. Laura, not able to imagine agency for herself, says far less than Jim. Varya says a bit more than Lopakhin, including the banal remark that ends the scene, and in a sense, her life: "Anyway, the thermometer's broken."

After she says this, someone calls to Lopakhin, and he runs away.

Coming as it does at the decisive moment, close to the end of a play that's filled with things being broken and smashed, Varya's simple remark about the thermometer carries little meaning when it's delivered, and a fatal resonance afterwards. A broken world is coming apart, past repair. After the old servant Firs, having been left behind by the departing aristocrats, dies sitting up, the last events in Chekhov's play are the offstage sound of a string snapping, and then the resumption of axes chopping down trees.

There's an echo of this snapping string in the notebook entry, quoted earlier, written immediately after Rose Williams's lobotomy: "A cord is breaking." It's unclear whether Tennessee meant, but misspelled, "chord," referring to broken musical chords, just as it's unclear what specifically Abraham Lincoln envisioned when he spoke of the "mystic chords of memory stretching from every battlefield and patriot grave." Whether cord or chord, guitar string or heartstrings, the bonds that unite human beings are as immaterial and durable as the laws of relationship that govern harmonics, as hard and as breakable as the invisible crystalline structure of glass.

On the third anniversary of the opening of *The Glass Menagerie*, Tennessee wrote an essay, "The Catastrophe of Success," which has been used ever since as an introduction to the play. In it he presented himself as so discombobulated by his accomplishment that he took refuge from it by going under the knife for cataract surgery, relocating his true self in his convalescence. It's nervy and risky for a newly successful writer to complain about the burdens of wealth and fame; it invites a critical, if not a popular backlash. Success may be ego-dystonic, but who wants to hear about it? If any notion of Tennessee Williams as a buckskin-clad backwoods primitive wasn't dispelled by *The Glass Menagerie*, the essay firmly placed the playwright in the ranks of physically afflicted sensitives, and there he would stubbornly, proudly remain. He proclaimed his physical weakness insistently, earning a lifelong reputation as a hypochondriac, one of a number of neuroses he not only didn't deny but merrily added to the list of things wrong with him that he regularly served up to interviewers.

And all the while he continued to perform wonders as an artist. He was an experimental as well as a commercial playwright, seeking, as he put it in his journal, the means with which to put on stage "apocalypse without delirium." Although his diction is unmistakable in all his plays, stories, and poems, and his concerns cohere across his enormous body of work, he never attempted to follow any success by merely repeating it. In his subsequent work he perfected the gestures of *Menagerie* and at the same time abandoned them, departing without ceremony from the kind of delicate memory play he'd invented, no further examples of which, he'd announced, could be anticipated from him; he left imitation of *The Glass Menagerie* to its many, many imitators. In the two years after *Menagerie,* he wrote an early version of the vast and loony *Camino Real,* finished *Summer and Smoke,* and moved on to the play for which Alma Winemiller and her stone angel had been merely a stepping-stone (albeit a beautiful stone, well worth stepping on). By the end of 1947 he'd opened *A Streetcar Named Desire.*

He branded himself—and sincerely believed himself to be—a neurasthenic hypochondriac and a neurotic in need of pity and tender care, while busily casting expectations and aesthetic and social conventions aside, exhibiting an exuberance and an output possible only from a person extraordinarily, robustly alive. Tennessee presented a bewildering, gaudy, fascinating spectacle, expressive of his contradictory relationship to power, to agency, to force. The public platform upon which this was staged was given to him as the reward for writing *The Glass Menagerie.* When he was writing *Menagerie,* not yet having earned a platform, having no secure perch, he hid his spectacle under a bushel. He could write about frailty, but not yet about desire. Hence the play's sexual reticence.

If he was afraid, he was wise to be. It didn't take long for the cultural police to put the pieces together and figure out that a fragile neurotic who wrote about women's sexual appetites in a language of lyric power never heard before in American theater was a homosexual, who, it was concluded, couldn't possibly understand or write about real women or about desires of interest to any but the diseased and perverted.

Fear of censure, however, can't explain much in Tennessee's determinedly public life of recklessness and courage. He wasn't a timid writer. He gave voice in *Menagerie* to what he understood, at the time, to be the near-total nature of Rose's powerlessness, of Laura's, of his own. Dedicating his talent and his art to the purpose of understanding and representing the power of the weak was an act of fierce, defiant solidarity, a political act. If there's an odor of fetishized suffering in his understanding, of masochism in his representation, it, too, is political in nature, in that it emanates from inaction, from an inability to see the possibility of change.

Tennessee was in Provincetown in the summer of 1944, at the same time as the poet Robert Duncan. Tennessee was completing *The Glass Menagerie*. Duncan had written an essay, "The Homosexual In Society," the publication of which, in that August's issue of Dwight Macdonald's *Politics*, is now recognized as a catalytic event in the formation of the gay liberation movement. Publicly, unapologetically declaring himself to be homosexual took enormous courage, and for decades afterwards Duncan paid the price for it.

The essay takes aback contemporary readers who come to it expecting a dated, nervous plea for tolerance. Like everything Duncan wrote, it's wildly original and challenging. Conforming to no party-building or even practical political sense, he began the essay by assuming, in a tone of irascible impatience that rarely lightens, a shared understanding of the ugly consequences of homophobia—an outrageous, or visionary, assumption to be making in 1944, or in 1964, or in 1984. Eschewing the accusatory brief and petition for redress that would have been the usual effort of a spokesman for a severely oppressed people, eschewing the role of spokesman, demonstrating little interest in oppressors or in petitionable authorities, Duncan brought his choleric intelligence to bear on the oppressed. He accused homosexuals, including himself, of participating in their own oppression by making a culture of weakness and powerlessness, by becoming obsessed with difference and failing to understand the universal aspect of their desires—no wonder a socialist journal accepted the essay. It was a disturbing performance, one which Duncan in later years cringed at, explicated, but never repudiated.

Apart from the simple fact of its appearance, "The Homosexual In Society" encouraged lesbians and gay men to organize and resist because Duncan so forcefully and persuasively assumed the inevitability of liberation, and constructed a call to arms predicated on the further assumption that the power to liberate lay not with the powerful but with those seeking liberation.

Tennessee and Duncan became friends, discussing Melville and Proust. Tennessee attended a reading of "The Homosexual In Society" given by Duncan that autumn in Manhattan, but no evidence has emerged as to what Tennessee made of it. Eventually Duncan formed a negative opinion of Tennessee's plays, according to his biographer Ekbert Faas, lamenting that a mediocre play like *Menagerie* had won accolades while a masterpiece like *The Iceman Cometh* had failed.

Did Tennessee feel implicated when listening to Duncan rail against poets in the grip of a "nostalgic picture of special worth in suffering, sensitivity"? Did he feel included in the company of the "modern ghouls" Duncan assailed who had "ravaged" "the body of [Hart] Crane and, once ravaged, stuck-up cult-wise in the mystic light of their special cemetery literature"?

Or did he hear, in Duncan's jeremiad, as he may have heard in Melville, and certainly heard in Proust, the sounds of a familiar tension and tearing, occasioned by the effort to forge a new relationship between the oppressed and power itself? Did he recognize a kindred struggle to redefine strength so as to produce new circumstances, a new world of freedom from oppression, rather than blindly to assume the habiliments, habits, and violence of oppressors?

Well, he certainly wouldn't have put it that way. But the voluble uneasiness in Duncan's essay, and the speaking silences in Tennessee's play, are manifestations of a new consciousness and a new language being born. It's easier to see this in Duncan, who, for a time, aspired to direct participation in politics. Tennessee never did, but that's not to say that his writing is apolitical. As has been noted, his ambitions were always politically charged, placing him in opposition to dominant American cultural values. But fidelity to the powerlessness he sought to dramatize made overtly, aggressively political art incommensurable with his subject, if not a betrayal of it.

Mention has already been made of the jarring bits of mid-century modernist theatrical experimentation scattered throughout the text of *The Glass Menagerie*, including listing of the characters as types, the use of slides of images and scene titles, and the absence of demarcated acts in the play, its division instead into a succession of numbered scenes (this is true of *Streetcar* as well). They're routinely ignored in production because employing them would damage the Chekhovian unity of color and mood Tennessee aspired to, the magical integration of lyricism and naturalism he'd originated in *Menagerie*.

These formal devices are alien visitations from the theater of Brecht, with which Tennessee would have been familiar through his brief connection with one of Brecht's chief influences, Erwin Piscator, who by the 1930s was teaching and directing at the New School in New York. There's a likely source as well in Thornton Wilder's 1938 *Our Town*, which borrowed—via Brecht, Piscator and the pre-Stalinist Russian theatrical and cinematic avant garde—the narrational techniques of Asian theater.

The slides, as well as the numbered and titled scenes in the text of *Menagerie*, might be regarded as markers of a buried political intention which the playwright was unable to assimilate into the tragedy of suspended action and of memory he was composing, but which he left behind as evidence of a dalliance with the theater of distanciation, reportage and collage, with the gestures of overtly political art.

The Glass Menagerie came into being and met its public during an extremely perilous, highly politicized time. Had *Menagerie* arrived in New York earlier in the war, rather than a month before VE Day, there might not have been an audience for a play of its intimate scale, in which concerns for mildly disabled girls and breakable glass figurines are given most of the available stage time, while the societal disintegration and global conflagration that are its context are relegated to brief, bookending poetic passages.

A play has to be in sync and in some kind of accord with its historical moment, answering some public need if it's to succeed. *Menagerie* was very nearly ahead of its time. It took weeks, the determination of two enthusiastic critics, and slowly building word-of-mouth about Laurette Taylor's performance to attract an audience in Chicago the year before. With the war ending, New York proclaimed it a hit from opening night, but Lewis Nichols, in his favorable review in *The New York Times*, complained that among the "good many flaws" to be found in the play were "unconnected odds and ends which have little to do with the story," including "snatches of talk about the war."

These snatches are in Tom's monologues. With Thorton Wilderish irony, Tom offers the audience what he calls the play's "social background," situating the Wingfields, their small apartment and small tragedy in a deeply troubled, darkening world, lit by lightning. Depression America is a land of blind people whose fingers are being forcibly pressed to the "fiery Braille of a dissolving economy." Tom isn't sure whether they're blind and being forced to suffer because "their eyes had failed them, or they had failed their eyes." Those who suffer, in other words, may be victims of malevolent circumstance, or its cause. It is emblematic of the play's relationship to politics that this conundrum of historical agency is presented; no solution or resolution is proposed, but it reverberates quietly in the play.

Through these magnificent snatches, Tennessee evokes politics, society and history, apprehending rather than comprehending their relationship to his beleaguered family; the connection between political and personal agony is intimated in lightning flashes rather than expounded upon at length. Jittery, hesitant, oblique and allusive, the play dramaturgically recapitulates the humanity it brings to dramatic life.

On September 26, 1943, Tennessee copied out a passage from *Journey Between Wars*, by E. E. Cummings's friend and war buddy John Dos Passos, in which the fate of the world is poised between brutal reality and illusion, between the powers of fragility and aggressive force, locked in life-or-death struggle.

How can the new world full of confusion and crosspurposes and illusions and dazzled by the mirage of idealistic phrases win against the iron combination of men accustomed to run things who have only one idea binding them together, to hold on to what they've got; how can the new world win?

Tennessee considered Dos Passos's question, and responds "[t]he answer is. We have got to straighten out. We will." He then teased himself for the fatuity of his response: "(Thank you, Mr. Williams, for solving that problem)," after which he offered an honest account of himself, which reads like an admission of defeat, a creed and a prayer. "My world is a world of a few simple ideas and a few simple feelings," he wrote, "to which I try to be faithful."

The power of intense fragility becomes perceptible only when connection, community is acknowledged. Its adversary is blunt, brutal individual strength, whose ambition is to dominate, to transform sociopathy into hegemony. Its triumphs depend on successfully denying that it depends on anything, on denying the existence of dependence and connection.

The theater, which exists only in the connections in which it traffics, only in community, is an ideal venue for the exploration of any ineffable. It is in the capacious shadows onstage that Tennessee sought, and found, a source of profound understanding and meaning.

"... I have never written a play that I thought was completed," he declared in a 1944 essay, "The History of a Play":

> and I don't think I ever will. There is too much to say and not enough time to say it. Nor is there power enough. I am not a good writer. Sometimes I am a very bad writer indeed. There is hardly a successful writer in the field who cannot write circles around me and I am first to admit it. But I think of writing as something more organized than words, something closer to being and action. I want to work more and more with a more plastic theater than the one that I have so far.

Tennessee possessed a deep-seated faith in the power of connection, even when all connection was obscured or obliterated from sight. He continues in the essay that he never doubted

> for one moment ... that there are people—millions!—to say things to. We come to each other gradually, but with love. It is the short reach of my arms that hinders, not the length and multiplicity of theirs. With love and honesty, the embrace is inevitable.

That's as lovely, brave, and beautiful an articulation of the artist's faith as any ever written. And that faith is the precondition of art's indirect power to change the world.

It is because of this faith, perhaps, that the first word spoken in *The Glass Menagerie* is "yes."

TONY KUSHNER

THE GLASS
MENAGERIE

nobody, not even the rain, has such small hands

E. E. Cummings

THE CHARACTERS

AMANDA WINGFIELD *(the mother)*

A little woman of great but confused vitality clinging frantically to another time and place. Her characterization must be carefully created, not copied from type. She is not paranoiac, but her life is paranoia. There is much to admire in Amanda, and as much to love and pity as there is to laugh at. Certainly she has endurance and a kind of heroism, and though her foolishness makes her unwittingly cruel at times, there is tenderness in her slight person.

LAURA WINGFIELD *(her daughter)*

Amanda, having failed to establish contact with reality, continues to live vitally in her illusions, but Laura's situation is even graver. A childhood illness has left her crippled, one leg slightly shorter than the other, and held in a brace. This defect need not be more than suggested on the stage. Stemming from this, Laura's separation increases till she is like a piece of her own glass collection, too exquisitely fragile to move from the shelf.

TOM WINGFIELD *(her son)*

And the narrator of the play. A poet with a job in a warehouse. His nature is not remorseless, but to escape from a trap he has to act without pity.

JIM O'CONNOR *(the gentleman caller)*

A nice, ordinary, young man.

CAST LISTING AND SCENE

The Glass Menagerie was first produced by Eddie Dowling and Louis J. Singer at the Civic Theatre, Chicago, Illinois, on December 26, 1944, and at the Playhouse Theatre, New York City, on March 31, 1945. The setting was designed and lighted by Jo Mielziner; original music was composed by Paul Bowles; the play was staged by Eddie Dowling and Margo Jones. The cast was as follows:

THE MOTHER	Laurette Taylor
HER SON	Eddie Dowling
HER DAUGHTER	Julie Haydon
THE GENTLEMAN CALLER	Anthony Ross

SCENE: *An alley in St. Louis*

TIME: *Now and the Past*

Part I. Preparation for a Gentleman Caller.

Part II. The Gentleman calls.

AUTHOR'S PRODUCTION NOTES

Being a "memory play," *The Glass Menagerie* can be presented with unusual freedom of convention. Because of its considerably delicate or tenuous material, atmospheric touches and subtleties of direction play a particularly important part. Expressionism and all other unconventional techniques in drama have only one valid aim, and that is a closer approach to truth. When a play employs unconventional techniques, it is not, or certainly shouldn't be, trying to escape its responsibility of dealing with reality, or interpreting experience, but is actually or should be attempting to find a closer approach, a more penetrating and vivid expression of things as they are. The straight realistic play with its genuine Frigidaire and authentic ice-cubes, its characters who speak exactly as its audience speaks, corresponds to the academic landscape and has the same virtue of a photographic likeness. Everyone should know nowadays the unimportance of the photographic in art: that truth, life, or reality is an organic thing which the poetic imagination can represent or suggest, in essence, only through transformation, through changing into other forms than those which were merely present in appearance.

These remarks are not meant as a preface only to this particular play. They have to do with a conception of a new, plastic theatre which must take the place of the exhausted theatre of realistic conventions if the theatre is to resume vitality as a part of our culture.

THE SCREEN DEVICE: There is *only one important difference between the original and the acting version of the play* and that is the *omission* in the latter of the device that I tentatively included in my *original* script. This device was the use of a screen on which were projected magic-lantern slides bearing images or titles. I do not regret the omission of this device from the original Broadway production. The extraordinary power of Miss Taylor's performance made it suitable to have the utmost simplicity in the physical production. But I think it may be interesting to some readers to see how this device was conceived. So I am putting it into the published manuscript. These images and legends, projected from behind, were cast on a section of wall between the front-room and dining-room areas, which should be indistinguishable from the rest when not in use.

The purpose of this will probably be apparent. It is to give accent to certain values in each scene. Each scene contains a particular point (or several) which is structurally the most important. In an episodic play, such as this, the basic structure or narrative line may be obscured from the audience; the effect may seem fragmentary rather than architectural. This may not be the fault of the play so much as a lack of attention in the audience. The legend or image upon the screen will strengthen the effect of what is merely allusion in the writing and allow the primary point to be made more simply and lightly than if the entire responsibility were on the spoken lines. Aside from this structural value, I think the screen will have a definite emotional appeal, less definable but just as important. An imaginative producer or director may invent many other uses for this device than those indicated in the present script. In fact the possibilities of the device seem much larger to me than the instance of this play can possibly utilize.

THE MUSIC: Another extra-literary accent in this play is provided by the use of music. A single recurring tune, "The Glass Menagerie," is used to give emotional emphasis to suitable passages. This tune is like circus music, not when you are on the grounds or in the immediate vicinity of the parade, but when you are at some distance and very likely thinking of something else. It seems under those circumstances to continue almost interminably and it weaves in and out of your preoccupied consciousness; then it is the lightest, most delicate music in the world and perhaps the saddest. It expresses the surface vivacity of life with the underlying strain of immutable and inexpressible sorrow. When you look at a piece of delicately spun glass you think of two things: how beautiful it is and how easily it can be broken. Both of those ideas should be woven into the recurring tune, which dips in and out of the play as if it were carried on a wind that changes. It serves as a thread of connection and allusion between the narrator with his separate point in time and space and the subject of his story. Between each episode it returns as reference to the emotion, nostalgia, which is the first condition of the play. It is primarily Laura's music and therefore comes out most clearly when the play focuses upon her and the lovely fragility of glass which is her image.

THE LIGHTING: The lighting in the play is not realistic. In keeping with the atmosphere of memory, the stage is dim. Shafts of light are focused on selected areas or actors, sometimes in contradistinction to what is the apparent center. For instance, in the quarrel scene between Tom and Amanda, in which Laura has no active part, the clearest pool of light is on her figure. This is also true of the supper scene, when her silent figure on the sofa should remain the visual center. The light upon Laura should be distinct from the others, having a peculiar pristine clarity such as light used in early religious portraits of female saints or madonnas. A certain correspondence to light in religious paintings, such as El Greco's, where the figures are radiant in atmosphere that is relatively dusky, could be effectively used throughout the play. (It will also permit a more effective use of the screen.) A free, imaginative use of light can be of enormous value in giving a mobile, plastic quality to plays of a more or less static nature.

TENNESSEE WILLIAMS

SCENE ONE

The Wingfield apartment is in the rear of the building, one of those vast hive-like conglomerations of cellular living-units that flower as warty growths in overcrowded urban centers of lower middle-class population and are symptomatic of the impulse of this largest and fundamentally enslaved section of American society to avoid fluidity and differentiation and to exist and function as one interfused mass of automatism.

The apartment faces an alley and is entered by a fire escape, a structure whose name is a touch of accidental poetic truth, for all of these huge buildings are always burning with the slow and implacable fires of human desperation. The fire escape is part of what we see—that is, the landing of it and steps descending from it.

The scene is memory and is therefore nonrealistic. Memory takes a lot of poetic license. It omits some details; others are exaggerated, according to the emotional value of the articles it touches, for memory is seated predominantly in the heart. The interior is therefore rather dim and poetic.

At the rise of the curtain, the audience is faced with the dark, grim rear wall of the Wingfield tenement. This building is flanked on both sides by dark, narrow alleys which run into murky canyons of tangled clotheslines, garbage cans, and the sinister latticework of neighboring fire escapes. It is up and down these side alleys that exterior entrances and exits are made during the play. At the end of Tom's opening commentary, the dark tenement wall slowly becomes transparent and reveals the interior of the ground-floor Wingfield apartment.

Nearest the audience is the living room, which also serves as a sleeping room for Laura, the sofa unfolding to make her bed. Just beyond, separated from the living room by a wide arch or second proscenium with transparent jaded portieres (or second curtain), is the dining room. In an old-fashioned whatnot in the living room are seen scores of transparent glass animals. A blown-up photograph of the father hangs on the wall of the living room, to the left of the archway. It is the face of a very handsome young man in a doughboy's First World War cap. He is gallantly smiling, ineluctably smiling, as if to say "I will be smiling forever."

Also hanging on the wall, near the photograph, are a typewriter keyboard chart and a Gregg shorthand diagram. An upright typewriter on a small table stands beneath the charts.

The audience hears and sees the opening scene in the dining room through both the transparent fourth wall of the building and the transparent gauze portieres of the dining-room arch. It is during this revealing scene that the fourth wall slowly ascends, out of sight. This transparent exterior wall is not brought down again until the very end of the play, during Tom's final speech.

The narrator is an undisguised convention of the play. He takes whatever license with dramatic convention is convenient to his purposes.

Tom enters, dressed as a merchant sailor, and strolls across to the fire escape. There he stops and lights a cigarette. He addresses the audience.

TOM: Yes, I have tricks in my pocket, I have things up my sleeve. But I am the opposite of a stage magician. He gives you illusion that has the appearance of truth. I give you truth in the pleasant disguise of illusion.

To begin with, I turn back time. I reverse it to that quaint period, the thirties, when the huge middle class of America was matriculating in a school for the blind. Their eyes had failed them, or they had failed their eyes, and so they were having their fingers pressed forcibly down on the fiery Braille alphabet of a dissolving economy.

In Spain there was revolution. Here there was only shouting

and confusion. In Spain there was Guernica. Here there were disturbances of labor, sometimes pretty violent, in otherwise peaceful cities such as Chicago, Cleveland, Saint Louis . . . This is the social background of the play.

[*Music begins to play.*]

The play is memory. Being a memory play, it is dimly lighted, it is sentimental, it is not realistic. In memory everything seems to happen to music. That explains the fiddle in the wings.

I am the narrator of the play, and also a character in it. The other characters are my mother, Amanda, my sister, Laura, and a gentleman caller who appears in the final scenes. He is the most realistic character in the play, being an emissary from a world of reality that we were somehow set apart from. But since I have a poet's weakness for symbols, I am using this character also as a symbol; he is the long-delayed but always expected something that we live for.

There is a fifth character in the play who doesn't appear except in this larger-than-life-size photograph over the mantel. This is our father who left us a long time ago. He was a telephone man who fell in love with long distances; he gave up his job with the telephone company and skipped the light fantastic out of town . . .

The last we heard of him was a picture postcard from Mazatlan, on the Pacific coast of Mexico, containing a message of two words: "Hello—Goodbye!" and no address.

I think the rest of the play will explain itself. . . .

[*Amanda's voice becomes audible through the portieres. Legend on screen: "Ou sont les neiges."* Tom divides the portieres and enters the dining room. Amanda and Laura are seated at a drop-leaf table. Eating is indicated by gestures without food or utensils. Amanda faces the audience. Tom and Laura are seated in profile. The interior has lit up softly and through the scrim we see Amanda and Laura seated at the table.]

AMANDA [*calling*]: Tom?

TOM: Yes, Mother.

AMANDA: We can't say grace until you come to the table!

TOM: Coming, Mother. [*He bows slightly and withdraws, reappearing a few moments later in his place at the table.*]

AMANDA [*to her son*]: Honey, don't *push* with your *fingers*. If you have to push with something, the thing to push with is a crust of bread. And chew—chew! Animals have secretions in their stomachs which enable them to digest food without mastication, but human beings are supposed to chew their food before they swallow it down. Eat food leisurely, son, and really enjoy it. A well-cooked meal has lots of delicate flavors that have to be held in the mouth for appreciation. So chew your food and give your salivary glands a chance to function!

[*Tom deliberately lays his imaginary fork down and pushes his chair back from the table.*]

TOM: I haven't enjoyed one bite of this dinner because of your constant directions on how to eat it. It's you that make me rush through meals with your hawklike attention to every bite I take. Sickening—spoils my appetite—all this discussion of—animals' secretion—salivary glands—mastication!

AMANDA [*lightly*]: Temperament like a Metropolitan star!

[*Tom rises and walks toward the living room.*]

You're not excused from the table.

TOM: I'm getting a cigarette.

AMANDA: You smoke too much.

[*Laura rises.*]

LAURA: I'll bring in the blancmange.

[*Tom remains standing with his cigarette by the portieres.*]

AMANDA [*rising*]: No, sister, no, sister—you be the lady this time and I'll be the darky.

LAURA: I'm already up.

AMANDA: Resume your seat, little sister—I want you to stay fresh and pretty—for gentlemen callers!

LAURA [*sitting down*]: I'm not expecting any gentlemen callers.

AMANDA [*crossing out to the kitchenette, airily*]: Sometimes they come when they are least expected! Why, I remember one Sunday afternoon in Blue Mountain— [*She enters the kitchenette.*]

TOM: I know what's coming!

LAURA: Yes. But let her tell it.

TOM: Again?

LAURA: She loves to tell it.

[*Amanda returns with a bowl of dessert*].

AMANDA: One Sunday afternoon in Blue Mountain—your mother received—*seventeen!*—gentlemen callers! Why, sometimes there weren't chairs enough to accommodate them all. We had to send the nigger over to bring in folding chairs from the parish house.

TOM [*remaining at the portieres*]: How did you entertain those gentlemen callers?

AMANDA: I understood the art of conversation!

TOM: I bet you could talk.

AMANDA: Girls in those days *knew* how to talk, I can tell you.

TOM: Yes?

[*Image on screen*: Amanda as a girl on a porch, greeting callers.]

AMANDA: They knew how to entertain their gentlemen callers. It wasn't enough for a girl to be possessed of a pretty face and a graceful figure—although I wasn't slighted in either respect. She also needed to have a nimble wit and a tongue to meet all occasions.

TOM: What did you talk about?

AMANDA: Things of importance going on in the world! Never anything coarse or common or vulgar.

[*She addresses Tom as though he were seated in the vacant chair at the table though he remains by the portieres. He plays this scene as though reading from a script.*]

My callers were gentlemen—all! Among my callers were some of the most prominent young planters of the Mississippi Delta—planters and sons of planters!

[*Tom motions for music and a spot of light on Amanda. Her eyes lift, her face glows, her voice becomes rich and elegiac. Screen legend*: "Ou sont les neiges d'antan?"]

There was young Champ Laughlin who later became vice-president of the Delta Planters Bank. Hadley Stevenson who was drowned in Moon Lake and left his widow one hundred and fifty thousand in Government bonds. There were the Cutrere brothers, Wesley and Bates. Bates was one of my bright particular beaux! He got in a quarrel with that wild Wainwright boy. They shot it out on the floor of Moon Lake Casino. Bates was shot through the stomach. Died in the ambulance on his way to Memphis. His widow was also well provided-for, came into eight or ten thousand acres, that's all. She married him on the rebound—never loved her—carried my picture on him the night he died! And there was that boy that every girl in the Delta had set her cap for! That beautiful, brilliant young

Fitzhugh boy from Greene County!

TOM: What did he leave his widow?

AMANDA: He never married! Gracious, you talk as though all of my old admirers had turned up their toes to the daisies!

TOM: Isn't this the first you've mentioned that still survives?

AMANDA: That Fitzhugh boy went North and made a fortune— came to be known as the Wolf of Wall Street! He had the Midas touch, whatever he touched turned to gold! And I could have been Mrs. Duncan J. Fitzhugh, mind you! But—I picked your *father!*

LAURA [*rising*]: Mother, let me clear the table.

AMANDA: No, dear, you go in front and study your typewriter chart. Or practice your shorthand a little. Stay fresh and pretty!— It's almost time for our gentlemen callers to start arriving. [*She flounces girlishly toward the kitchenette.*] How many do you suppose we're going to entertain this afternoon?

[*Tom throws down the paper and jumps up with a groan.*]

LAURA [*alone in the dining room*]: I don't believe we're going to receive any, Mother.

AMANDA [*reappearing, airily*]: What? No one—not one? You must be joking!

[*Laura nervously echoes her laugh. She slips in a fugitive manner through the half-open portieres and draws them gently behind her. A shaft of very clear light is thrown on her face against the faded tapestry of the curtains. Faintly the music of "The Glass Menagerie" is heard as Amanda continues, lightly.*]

Not one gentleman caller? It can't be true! There must be a flood, there must have been a tornado!

LAURA: It isn't a flood, it's not a tornado, Mother. I'm just not popular like you were in Blue Mountain. . . .

[*Tom utters another groan. Laura glances at him with a faint, apologetic smile. Her voice catches a little.*]

Mother's afraid I'm going to be an old maid.

[*The scene dims out with the "Glass Menagerie" music.*]

SCENE TWO

On the dark stage the screen is lighted with the image of blue roses. Gradually Laura's figure becomes apparent and the screen goes out. The music subsides.

Laura is seated in the delicate ivory chair at the small claw-foot table. She wears a dress of soft violet material for a kimono—her hair is tied back from her forehead with a ribbon. She is washing and polishing her collection of glass. Amanda appears on the fire escape steps. At the sound of her ascent, Laura catches her breath, thrusts the bowl of ornaments away, and seats herself stiffly before the diagram of the typewriter keyboard as though it held her spellbound. Something has happened to Amanda. It is written in her face as she climbs to the landing: a look that is grim and hopeless and a little absurd. She has on one of those cheap or imitation velvety-looking cloth coats with imitation fur collar. Her hat is five or six years old, one of those dreadful cloche hats that were worn in the late Twenties, and she is clutching an enormous black patent-leather pocketbook with nickel clasps and initials. This is her full-dress outfit, the one she usually wears to the D.A.R. Before entering she looks through the door. She purses her lips, opens her eyes very wide, rolls them upward and shakes her head. Then she slowly lets herself in the door. Seeing her mother's expression Laura touches her lips with a nervous gesture.

LAURA: Hello, Mother, I was— [*She makes a nervous gesture toward the chart on the wall. Amanda leans against the shut door and stares at Laura with a martyred look.*]

AMANDA: Deception? Deception? [*She slowly removes her hat and gloves, continuing the sweet suffering stare. She lets the hat and gloves fall on the floor—a bit of acting.*]

LAURA [*shakily*]: How was the D.A.R. meeting?

[*Amanda slowly opens her purse and removes a dainty white handkerchief which she shakes out delicately and delicately touches to her lips and nostrils.*]

Didn't you go to the D.A.R. meeting, Mother?

AMANDA [*faintly, almost inaudibly*]: —No.—No. [*Then more forcibly.*] I did not have the strength—to go to the D.A.R. In fact, I did not have the courage! I wanted to find a hole in the ground and hide myself in it forever! [*She crosses slowly to the wall and removes the diagram of the typewriter keyboard. She holds it in front of her for a second, staring at it sweetly and sorrowfully— then bites her lips and tears it in two pieces.*]

LAURA [*faintly*]: Why did you do that, Mother?

[*Amanda repeats the same procedure with the chart of the Gregg Alphabet.*]

Why are you—

AMANDA: Why? Why? How old are you, Laura?

LAURA: Mother, you know my age.

AMANDA: I thought that you were an adult; it seems that I was mistaken. [*She crosses slowly to the sofa and sinks down and stares at Laura.*]

LAURA: Please don't stare at me, Mother.

[*Amanda closes her eyes and lowers her head. There is a ten-second pause.*]

AMANDA: What are we going to do, what is going to become of us, what is the future?

[*There is another pause.*]

LAURA: Has something happened, Mother?

[*Amanda draws a long breath, takes out the handkerchief again, goes through the dabbing process.*]

Mother, has—something happened?

AMANDA: I'll be all right in a minute, I'm just bewildered— [*She hesitates.*] —by life. . . .

LAURA: Mother, I wish that you would tell me what's happened!

AMANDA: As you know, I was supposed to be inducted into my office at the D.A.R. this afternoon.

[*Screen image*: A swarm of typewriters.]

But I stopped off at Rubicam's Business College to speak to your teachers about your having a cold and ask them what progress they thought you were making down there.

LAURA: Oh. . . .

AMANDA: I went to the typing instructor and introduced myself as your mother. She didn't know who you were. "Wingfield," she said, "We don't have any such student enrolled at the school!" I assured her she did, that you had been going to classes since early in January.

"I wonder," she said, "If you could be talking about that terribly shy little girl who dropped out of school after only a few days' attendance?"

"No," I said, "Laura, my daughter, has been going to school every day for the past six weeks!"

"Excuse me," she said. She took the attendance book out and there was your name, unmistakably printed, and all the dates you were absent until they decided that you had dropped out of school.

I still said, "No, there must have been some mistake! There must have been some mix-up in the records!"

And she said, "No—I remember her perfectly now. Her hands

shook so that she couldn't hit the right keys! The first time we gave a speed test, she broke down completely—was sick at the stomach and almost had to be carried into the wash room! After that morning she never showed up any more. We phoned the house but never got any answer"— While I was working at Famous–Barr, I suppose, demonstrating those— [*She indicates a brassiere with her hands.*] Oh! I felt so weak I could barely keep on my feet! I had to sit down while they got me a glass of water! Fifty dollars' tuition, all of our plans—my hopes and ambitions for you—just gone up the spout, just gone up the spout like that.

[*Laura draws a long breath and gets awkwardly to her feet. She crosses to the Victrola and winds it up.*]

What are you doing?

LAURA: Oh! [*She releases the handle and returns to her seat.*]

AMANDA: Laura, where have you been going when you've gone out pretending that you were going to business college?

LAURA: I've just been going out walking.

AMANDA: That's not true.

LAURA: It is. I just went walking.

AMANDA: Walking? Walking? In winter? Deliberately courting pneumonia in that light coat? Where did you walk to, Laura?

LAURA: All sorts of places—mostly in the park.

AMANDA: Even after you'd started catching that cold?

LAURA: It was the lesser of two evils, Mother.

[*Screen image*: Winter scene in a park.]

I couldn't go back there. I—threw up—on the floor!

AMANDA: From half past seven till after five every day you mean to tell me you walked around in the park, because you wanted to make me think that you were still going to Rubicam's Business College?

LAURA: It wasn't as bad as it sounds. I went inside places to get warmed up.

AMANDA: Inside where?

LAURA: I went in the art museum and the bird houses at the Zoo. I visited the penguins every day! Sometimes I did without lunch and went to the movies. Lately I've been spending most of my afternoons in the Jewel Box, that big glass house where they raise the tropical flowers.

AMANDA: You did all this to deceive me, just for deception? [*Laura looks down.*] Why?

LAURA: Mother, when you're disappointed, you get that awful suffering look on your face, like the picture of Jesus' mother in the museum!

AMANDA: Hush!

LAURA: I couldn't face it.

[*There is a pause. A whisper of strings is heard. Legend on screen*: "The Crust of Humility."]

AMANDA [*hopelessly fingering the huge pocketbook*]: So what are we going to do the rest of our lives? Stay home and watch the parades go by? Amuse ourselves with the glass menagerie, darling? Eternally play those worn-out phonograph records your father left as a painful reminder of him? We won't have a business career— we've given that up because it gave us nervous indigestion! [*She laughs wearily.*] What is there left but dependency all our lives? I know so well what becomes of unmarried women who aren't prepared to occupy a position. I've seen such pitiful cases in the South—barely tolerated spinsters living upon the grudging patronage of sister's husband or brother's wife!—stuck away in some little mousetrap of a room—encouraged by one in-law to visit another—little birdlike women without any nest—eating the crust of humility all their life! Is that the future that we've mapped out for ourselves? I swear it's the only alternative I can think of! [*She pauses.*] It isn't a very pleasant alternative, is it? [*She pauses again.*] Of course—some girls *do marry.*

[*Laura twists her hands nervously.*]

Haven't you ever liked some boy?

LAURA: Yes. I liked one once. [*She rises.*] I came across his picture a while ago.

AMANDA [*with some interest*]: He gave you his picture?

LAURA: No, it's in the yearbook.

AMANDA [*disappointed*]: Oh—a high school boy.

[*Screen image*: Jim as the high school hero bearing a silver cup.]

LAURA: Yes. His name was Jim. [*She lifts the heavy annual from the claw-foot table.*] Here he is in *The Pirates of Penzance.*

AMANDA [*absently*]: The what?

LAURA: The operetta the senior class put on. He had a wonderful voice and we sat across the aisle from each other Mondays, Wednesdays and Fridays in the auditorium. Here he is with the silver cup for debating! See his grin?

AMANDA [*absently*]: He must have had a jolly disposition.

LAURA: He used to call me—Blue Roses.

[*Screen image*: Blue roses.]

AMANDA: Why did he call you such a name as that?

LAURA: When I had that attack of pleurosis—he asked me what was the matter when I came back. I said pleurosis—he thought that I said Blue Roses! So that's what he always called me after that. Whenever he saw me, he'd holler, "Hello, Blue Roses!" I didn't care for the girl that he went out with. Emily Meisenbach. Emily was the best-dressed girl at Soldan. She never struck me, though, as being sincere . . . It says in the Personal Section—they're engaged. That's—six years ago! They must be married by now.

AMANDA: Girls that aren't cut out for business careers usually wind up married to some nice man. [*She gets up with a spark of revival.*] Sister, that's what you'll do!

[*Laura utters a startled, doubtful laugh. She reaches quickly for a piece of glass.*]

LAURA: But, Mother—

AMANDA: Yes? [*She goes over to the photograph of Mr. Wingfield.*]

LAURA [*in a tone of frightened apology*]: I'm—crippled!

AMANDA: Nonsense! Laura, I've told you never, never to use that word. Why, you're not crippled, you just have a little defect—hardly noticeable, even! When people have some slight disadvantage like that, they cultivate other things to make up for it—develop charm—and vivacity—and—*charm!* That's all you have to do! [*She turns again to the photograph.*] One thing your father had plenty of—was *charm!*

[*The scene fades out with music.*]

SCENE THREE

TOM: After the fiasco at Rubicam's Business College, the idea of getting a gentleman caller for Laura began to play a more and more important part in Mother's calculations. It became an obsession. Like some archetype of the universal unconscious, the image of the gentleman caller haunted our small apartment. . . .

[*Screen image*: A young man at the door of a house with flowers.]

An evening at home rarely passed without some allusion to this image, this specter, this hope. . . . Even when he wasn't mentioned, his presence hung in Mother's preoccupied look and in my sister's frightened, apologetic manner—hung like a sentence passed upon the Wingfields!

Mother was a woman of action as well as words. She began to take logical steps in the planned direction. Late that winter and in the early spring—realizing that extra money would be needed to properly feather the nest and plume the bird—she conducted a vigorous campaign on the telephone, roping in subscribers to one of those magazines for matrons called *The Homemaker's Companion,* the type of journal that features the serialized sublimations of ladies of letters who think in terms of delicate cuplike breasts, slim, tapering waists, rich, creamy thighs, eyes like wood smoke in autumn, fingers that soothe and caress like strains of music, bodies as powerful as Etruscan sculpture.

[*Screen image*: The cover of a glamour magazine. *Amanda enters with the telephone on a long extension cord. She is spotlighted in the dim stage.*]

AMANDA: Ida Scott? This is Amanda Wingfield! We *missed* you at the D.A.R. last Monday! I said to myself: She's probably suffering with that sinus condition! How is that sinus condition? Horrors! Heaven have mercy!—You're a Christian martyr, yes, that's what you are, a Christian martyr! Well, I just now happened to notice that your subscription to the *Companion*'s about to expire! Yes, it expires with the next issue, honey!—just when that wonderful new serial by Bessie Mae Hopper is getting off to such an exciting start. Oh, honey, it's something that you can't miss! You remember how *Gone with the Wind* took everybody by storm? You simply couldn't go out if you hadn't read it. All everybody *talked* was Scarlett O'Hara. Well, this is a book that critics already compare to *Gone with the Wind*. It's the *Gone with the Wind* of the post-World-War generation! —What? —Burning? —Oh, honey, don't let them burn, go take a look in the oven and I'll hold the wire! Heavens—I think she's hung up!

[*The scene dims out. Legend on screen: "You think I'm in love with Continental Shoemakers?" Before the lights come up again, the violent voices of Tom and Amanda are heard. They are quarreling behind the portieres. In front of them stands Laura with clenched hands and panicky expression. A clear pool of light is on her figure throughout this scene.*]

TOM: What in Christ's name am I—

AMANDA [*shrilly*]: Don't you use that—

TOM: —supposed to do!

AMANDA: —expression! Not in my—

TOM: Ohhh!

AMANDA: —presence! Have you gone out of your senses?

TOM: I have, that's true, *driven* out!

AMANDA: What is the matter with you, you—big—big—IDIOT!

TOM: Look!—I've got *no thing,* no single thing—

AMANDA: Lower your voice!

TOM: —in my life here that I can call my OWN! Everything is—

AMANDA: Stop that shouting!

TOM: Yesterday you confiscated my books! You had the nerve to—

AMANDA: I took that horrible novel back to the library—yes! That hideous book by that insane Mr. Lawrence. [*Tom laughs wildly.*] I cannot control the output of diseased minds or people who cater to them— [*Tom laughs still more wildly.*] BUT I WON'T ALLOW SUCH FILTH BROUGHT INTO MY HOUSE! No, no, no, no, no!

TOM: House, house! Who pays rent on it, who makes a slave of himself to—

AMANDA [*fairly screeching*]: Don't you DARE to—

TOM: No, no, *I* mustn't say things! *I've* got to just—

AMANDA: Let me tell you—

TOM: I don't want to hear any more!

[*He tears the portieres open. The dining-room area is lit with a turgid smoky red glow. Now we see Amanda; her hair is in metal curlers and she is wearing a very old bathrobe, much too large for her slight figure, a relic of the faithless Mr. Wingfield. The upright typewriter now stands on the drop-leaf table, along with a wild disarray of manuscripts. The quarrel was probably precipitated by Amanda's interruption of Tom's creative labor. A chair lies overthrown on the floor. Their gesticulating shadows are cast on the ceiling by the fiery glow.*]

AMANDA: You *will* hear more, you—

TOM: No, I won't hear more, I'm going out!

AMANDA: You come right back in—

TOM: Out, out, out! Because I'm—

AMANDA: Come back here, Tom Wingfield! I'm not through talking to you!

TOM: Oh, go—

LAURA [*desperately*]: —Tom!

AMANDA: You're going to listen, and no more insolence from you! I'm at the end of my patience!

[*He comes back toward her.*]

TOM: What do you think I'm at? Aren't I supposed to have any patience to reach the end of, Mother? I know, I know. It seems unimportant to you, what I'm *doing*—what I *want* to do—having a little *difference* between them! You don't think that—

AMANDA: I think you've been doing things that you're ashamed of. That's why you act like this. I don't believe that you go every night to the movies. Nobody goes to the movies night after night. Nobody in their right minds goes to the movies as often as you pretend to. People don't go to the movies at nearly midnight, and movies don't let out at two A.M. Come in stumbling. Muttering to yourself like a maniac! You get three hours' sleep and then go to work. Oh, I can picture the way you're doing down there. Moping, doping, because you're in no condition.

TOM [*wildly*]: No, I'm in no condition!

AMANDA: What right have you got to jeopardize your job? Jeopardize the security of us all? How do you think we'd manage if you were—

TOM: Listen! You think I'm crazy about the *warehouse?* [*He bends fiercely toward her slight figure.*] You think I'm in love with the Continental Shoemakers? You think I want to spend fifty-five *years* down there in that—*celotex interior!* with—*fluorescent— tubes!* Look! I'd rather somebody picked up a crowbar and battered out my brains—than go back mornings! I *go!* Every time you come in yelling that Goddamn *"Rise and Shine!" "Rise and Shine!"* I say to myself, "How *lucky dead* people are!" But I get up. I *go!* For sixty-five dollars a month I give up all that I dream of doing and being *ever!* And you say self—*self's* all I ever think of. Why, listen, if self is what I thought of, Mother, I'd be where he is—GONE! [*He points to his father's picture.*] As far as the system of transportation reaches! [*He starts past her. She grabs his arm.*] Don't grab at me, Mother!

AMANDA: Where are you going?

TOM: I'm going to the *movies!*

AMANDA: I don't believe that lie!

[*Tom crouches toward her, overtowering her tiny figure. She backs away, gasping.*]

TOM: I'm going to opium dens! Yes, opium dens, dens of vice and criminals' hangouts, Mother. I've joined the Hogan Gang, I'm a hired assassin, I carry a tommy gun in a violin case! I run a string of cat houses in the Valley! They call me Killer, Killer Wingfield, I'm leading a double-life, a simple, honest warehouse worker by day, by night a dynamic *czar* of the *underworld, Mother.* I go to gambling casinos, I spin away fortunes on the roulette table! I wear a patch over one eye and a false mustache, sometimes I put on green whiskers. On those occasions they call me—*El Diablo!* Oh, I could tell you many things to make you sleepless! My enemies plan to dynamite this place. They're going to blow us all sky-high some night! I'll be glad, very happy, and so will you! You'll go up, up on a broomstick, over Blue Mountain with seventeen gentlemen callers! You ugly—babbling old—*witch.* . . . [*He goes through a series of violent, clumsy movements, seizing his overcoat, lunging to the door, pulling it fiercely open. The women watch him, aghast. His arm catches in the sleeve of the coat as he struggles to pull it on. For a moment he is pinioned by the bulky garment. With an outraged groan he tears the coat off again, splitting the shoulder of it, and hurls it across the room. It strikes against the shelf of Laura's glass collection, and there is a tinkle of shattering glass. Laura cries out as if wounded.*]

[*Music. Screen legend:* "The Glass Menagerie."]

LAURA [*shrilly*]: My glass!—menagerie. . . . [*She covers her face and turns away.*]

[*But Amanda is still stunned and stupefied by the "ugly witch" so that she barely notices this occurrence. Now she recovers her speech.*]

AMANDA [*in an awful voice*]: I won't speak to you—until you apologize!

[*She crosses through the portieres and draws them together behind her. Tom is left with Laura. Laura clings weakly to the mantel with her face averted. Tom stares at her stupidly for a moment. Then he crosses to the shelf. He drops awkwardly on his knees to collect the fallen glass, glancing at Laura as if he would speak but couldn't. "The Glass Menagerie" music steals in as the scene dims out.*]

SCENE FOUR

The interior of the apartment is dark. There is a faint light in the alley. A deep-voiced bell in a church is tolling the hour of five.

Tom appears at the top of the alley. After each solemn boom of the bell in the tower, he shakes a little noisemaker or rattle as if to express the tiny spasm of man in contrast to the sustained power and dignity of the Almighty. This and the unsteadiness of his advance make it evident that he has been drinking. As he climbs the few steps to the fire escape landing light steals up inside, Laura appears in the front room in a nightdress. She notices that Tom's bed is empty. Tom fishes in his pockets for his door key, removing a motley assortment of articles in the search, including a shower of movie ticket stubs and an empty bottle. At last he finds the key, but just as he is about to insert it, it slips from his fingers. He strikes a match and crouches below the door.

TOM [*bitterly*]: One crack—and it falls through!

[*Laura opens the door.*]

LAURA: Tom! Tom, what are you doing?

TOM: Looking for a door key.

LAURA: Where have you been all this time?

TOM: I have been to the movies.

LAURA: All this time at the movies?

TOM: There was a very long program. There was a Garbo picture and a Mickey Mouse and a travelogue and a newsreel and a preview of coming attractions. And there was an organ solo and a collection for the Milk Fund—simultaneously—which ended up in a terrible fight between a fat lady and an usher!

LAURA [*innocently*]: Did you have to stay through everything?

TOM: Of course! And, oh, I forgot! There was a big stage show! The headliner on this stage show was Malvolio the Magician. He performed wonderful tricks, many of them, such as pouring water back and forth between pitchers. First it turned to wine and then it turned to beer and then it turned to whisky. I know it was whisky it finally turned into because he needed somebody to come up out of the audience to help him, and I came up—both shows! It was Kentucky Straight Bourbon. A very generous fellow, he gave souvenirs. [*He pulls from his back pocket a shimmering rainbow-colored scarf.*] He gave me this. This is his magic scarf. You can have it, Laura. You wave it over a canary cage and you get a bowl of goldfish. You wave it over the goldfish bowl and they fly away canaries. . . . But the wonderfullest trick of all was the coffin trick. We nailed him into a coffin and he got out of the coffin without removing one nail. [*He has come inside.*] There is a trick that would come in handy for me—get me out of this two-by-four situation! [*He flops onto the bed and starts removing his shoes.*]

LAURA: Tom—shhh!

TOM: What're you shushing me for?

LAURA: You'll wake up Mother.

TOM: Goody, goody! Pay 'er back for all those "Rise an' Shines." [*He lies down, groaning.*] You know it don't take much intelligence to get yourself into a nailed-up coffin, Laura. But who in hell ever got himself out of one without removing one nail?

[*As if in answer, the father's grinning photograph lights up. The scene dims out. Immediately following, the church bell is heard striking six. At the sixth stroke the alarm clock goes off in Amanda's room, and after a few moments we hear her calling.*]

AMANDA [*offstage*]: Rise and Shine! Rise and Shine! Laura, go tell your brother to rise and shine!

TOM [*sitting up slowly*]: I'll rise—but I won't shine.

[*The light increases.*]

AMANDA [*offstage*]: Laura, tell your brother his coffee is ready.

[*Laura slips into the front room.*]

LAURA: Tom!—It's nearly seven. Don't make Mother nervous.

[*He stares at her stupidly.*]

[*Beseechingly.*] Tom, speak to Mother this morning. Make up with her, apologize, speak to her!

TOM: She won't to me. It's her that started not speaking.

LAURA: If you just say you're sorry she'll start speaking.

TOM: Her not speaking—is that such a tragedy?

LAURA: Please—please!

AMANDA [*calling from the kitchenette*]: Laura, are you going to do what I asked you to do, or do I have to get dressed and go out myself?

LAURA: Going, going—soon as I get on my coat! [*She pulls on a shapeless felt hat with a nervous, jerky movement, pleadingly glancing at Tom. She rushes awkwardly for her coat. The coat is one of Amanda's, inaccurately made-over, the sleeves too short for Laura.*] Butter and what else?

AMANDA [*entering from the kitchenette*]: Just butter. Tell them to charge it.

LAURA: Mother, they make such faces when I do that.

AMANDA: Sticks and stones can break our bones, but the expression on Mr. Garfinkel's face won't harm us! Tell your brother his coffee is getting cold.

LAURA [*at the door*]: Do what I asked you, will you, will you, Tom?

[*He looks sullenly away.*]

AMANDA: Laura, go now or just don't go at all!

LAURA [*rushing out*]: Going—going!

[*A second later she cries out. Tom springs up and crosses to the door. Tom opens the door.*]

TOM: Laura?

LAURA: I'm all right. I slipped, but I'm all right.

AMANDA [*peering anxiously after her*]: If anyone breaks a leg on those fire-escape steps, the landlord ought to be sued for every cent he possesses! [*She shuts the door. Now she remembers she isn't speaking to Tom and returns to the other room.*]

[*As Tom comes listlessly for his coffee, she turns her back to him and stands rigidly facing the window on the gloomy gray vault of the areaway, its light on her face with its aged but childish features is cruelly sharp, satirical as a Daumier print. The music of "Ave Maria," is heard softly. Tom glances sheepishly but sullenly at her averted figure and slumps at the table. The coffee is scalding hot; he sips it and gasps and spits it back in the cup. At his gasp, Amanda catches her breath and half turns. Then she catches herself and turns back to the window. Tom blows on his coffee, glancing sidewise at his mother. She clears her throat. Tom clears his. He starts to rise, sinks back down again, scratches his head, clears his throat again. Amanda coughs. Tom raises his cup*] *in both hands to blow on it, his eyes staring over the rim of it at his mother for several moments. Then he slowly sets the cup down and awkwardly and hesitantly rises from the chair.*]

TOM [*hoarsely*]: Mother. I—I apologize, Mother.

[*Amanda draws a quick, shuddering breath. Her face works grotesquely. She breaks into childlike tears.*]

I'm sorry for what I said, for everything that I said, I didn't mean it.

AMANDA [*sobbingly*]: My devotion has made me a witch and so I make myself hateful to my children!

TOM: *No,* you *don't.*

AMANDA: I worry so much, don't sleep, it makes me nervous!

TOM [*gently*]: I understand that.

AMANDA: I've had to put up a solitary battle all these years. But you're my right-hand bower! Don't fall down, don't fail!

TOM [*gently*]: I try, Mother.

AMANDA [*with great enthusiasm*]: Try and you will *succeed!* [*The notion makes her breathless.*] Why, you—you're just *full* of natural endowments! Both of my children—they're *unusual* children! Don't you think I know it? I'm so—*proud!* Happy and—feel I've—so much to be thankful for but—promise me one thing, son!

TOM: What, Mother?

AMANDA: Promise, son, you'll—never be a drunkard!

TOM [*turns to her grinning*]: I will never be a drunkard, Mother.

AMANDA: That's what frightened me so, that you'd be drinking! Eat a bowl of Purina!

TOM: Just coffee, Mother.

AMANDA: Shredded wheat biscuit?

TOM: No. No, Mother, just coffee.

AMANDA: You can't put in a day's work on an empty stomach. You've got ten minutes—don't gulp! Drinking too-hot liquids makes cancer of the stomach. . . . Put cream in.

TOM: No, thank you.

AMANDA: To cool it.

TOM: No! No, thank you, I want it black.

AMANDA: I know, but it's not good for you. We have to do all that we can to build ourselves up. In these trying times we live in, all that we have to cling to is—each other. . . . That's why it's so important to— Tom, I— I sent out your sister so I could discuss something with you. If you hadn't spoken I would have spoken to you. [*She sits down.*]

TOM [*gently*]: What is it, Mother, that you want to discuss?

AMANDA: *Laura!*

[*Tom puts his cup down slowly. Legend on screen*: "Laura." *Music*: "The Glass Menagerie."]

TOM: —Oh. —Laura . . .

AMANDA [*touching his sleeve*]: You know how Laura is. So quiet but—still water runs deep! She notices things and I think she—broods about them.

[*Tom looks up.*]

A few days ago I came in and she was crying.

TOM: What about?

AMANDA: You.

TOM: Me?

AMANDA: She has an idea that you're not happy here.

TOM: What gave her that idea?

AMANDA: What gives her any idea? However, you do act strangely. I—I'm not criticizing, understand *that!* I know your ambitions do not lie in the warehouse, that like everybody in the whole wide world—you've had to—make sacrifices, but—Tom—Tom—life's not easy, it calls for—Spartan endurance! There's so many things in my heart that I cannot describe to you! I've never told you but I—*loved* your father. . . .

TOM [*gently*]: I know that, Mother.

AMANDA: And you—when I see you taking after his ways! Staying out late—and—well, you *had* been drinking the night you were in that—terrifying condition! Laura says that you hate the apartment and that you go out nights to get away from it! Is that true, Tom?

TOM: No. You say there's so much in your heart that you can't describe to me. That's true of me, too. There's so much in my heart that I can't describe to *you!* So let's respect each other's—

AMANDA: But, why—*why*, Tom—are you always so *restless?* Where do you *go* to, nights?

TOM: I—go to the movies.

AMANDA: Why do you go to the movies so much, Tom?

TOM: I go to the movies because—I like adventure. Adventure is something I don't have much of at work, so I go to the movies.

AMANDA: But, Tom, you go to the movies *entirely* too *much!*

TOM: I like a lot of adventure.

[*Amanda looks baffled, then hurt. As the familiar inquisition resumes, Tom becomes hard and impatient again. Amanda slips back into her querulous attitude toward him. Image on screen: A sailing vessel with Jolly Roger.*]

AMANDA: Most young men find adventure in their careers.

TOM: Then most young men are not employed in a warehouse.

AMANDA: The world is full of young men employed in warehouses and offices and factories.

TOM: Do all of them find adventure in their careers?

AMANDA: They do or they do without it! Not everybody has a craze for adventure.

TOM: Man is by instinct a lover, a hunter, a fighter, and none of those instincts are given much play at the warehouse!

AMANDA: Man is by instinct! Don't quote instinct to me! Instinct is something that people have got away from! It belongs to animals! Christian adults don't want it!

TOM: What do Christian adults want, then, Mother?

AMANDA: Superior things! Things of the mind and the spirit! Only animals have to satisfy instincts! Surely your aims are somewhat higher than theirs! Than monkeys—pigs—

TOM: I reckon they're not.

AMANDA: You're joking. However, that isn't what I wanted to discuss.

TOM [*rising*]: I haven't much time.

AMANDA [*pushing his shoulders*]: Sit down.

TOM: You want me to punch in red at the warehouse, Mother?

AMANDA: You have five minutes. I want to talk about Laura.

[*Screen legend*: "Plans and Provisions."]

TOM: All right! What about Laura?

AMANDA: We have to be making some plans and provisions for her. She's older than you, two years, and nothing has happened. She just drifts along doing nothing. It frightens me terribly how she just drifts along.

TOM: I guess she's the type that people call home girls.

AMANDA: There's no such type, and if there is, it's a pity! That is unless the home is hers, with a husband!

TOM: What?

AMANDA: Oh, I can see the handwriting on the wall as plain as I see the nose in front of my face! It's terrify`ing! More and more you remind me of your father! He was out all hours without explanation!— Then *left! Goodbye!* And me with the bag to hold. I saw that letter you got from the Merchant Marine. I know what you're dreaming of. I'm not standing here blindfolded. [*She pauses.*] Very well, then. Then *do* it! But not till there's somebody to take your place.

TOM: What do you mean?

AMANDA: I mean that as soon as Laura has got somebody to take care of her, married, a home of her own, independent—why, then you'll be free to go wherever you please, on land, on sea, whichever way the wind blows you! But until that time you've got to look out for your sister. I don't say me because I'm old and don't matter! I say for your sister because she's young and dependent.

I put her in business college—a dismal failure! Frightened her so it made her sick at the stomach. I took her over to the Young People's League at the church. Another fiasco. She spoke to nobody, nobody spoke to her. Now all she does is fool with those pieces of glass and play those worn-out records. What kind of a life is that for a girl to lead?

TOM: What can I do about it?

AMANDA: Overcome selfishness! Self, self, self is all that you ever think of!

[*Tom springs up and crosses to get his coat. It is ugly and bulky. He pulls on a cap with earmuffs.*]

Where is your muffler? Put your wool muffler on!

[*He snatches it angrily from the closet, tosses it around his neck and pulls both ends tight.*]

Tom! I haven't said what I had in mind to ask you.

TOM: I'm too late to—

AMANDA [*catching his arm—very importunately; then shyly*]: Down at the warehouse, aren't there some—nice young men?

TOM: No!

AMANDA: There *must* be—*some* . . .

TOM: Mother— [*He gestures.*]

AMANDA: Find out one that's clean-living—doesn't drink and ask him out for sister!

TOM: What?

AMANDA: For *sister!* To *meet!* Get *acquainted!*

TOM [*stamping to the door*]: Oh, my *go-osh!*

AMANDA: Will you?

[*He opens the door. She says, imploringly:*]

Will you?

[*He starts down the fire escape.*]

Will you? *Will* you, dear?

TOM [*calling back*]: Yes!

[*Amanda closes the door hesitantly and with a troubled but faintly hopeful expression. Screen image*: The cover of a glamour magazine. *The spotlight picks up Amanda at the phone.*]

AMANDA: Ella Cartwright? This is Amanda Wingfield! How are you, honey? How is that kidney condition? [*There is a five-second pause.*] Horrors! [*There is another pause.*] You're a Christian martyr, yes, honey, that's what you are, a Christian martyr! Well, I just now happened to notice in my little red book that your subscription to the *Companion* has just run out! I knew that you wouldn't want to miss out on the wonderful serial starting in this new issue. It's by Bessie Mae Hopper, the first thing she's written since *Honeymoon for Three*. Wasn't that a strange and interesting story? Well, this one is even lovelier, I believe. It has a sophisticated, society background. It's all about the horsey set on Long Island!

[*The light fades out.*]

Legend on the screen: "Annunciation." *Music is heard as the light slowly comes on. It is early dusk of a spring evening. Supper has just been finished in the Wingfield apartment. Amanda and Laura, in light-colored dresses, are removing dishes from the table in the dining room, which is shadowy, their movements formalized almost as a dance or ritual, their moving forms as pale and silent as moths. Tom, in white shirt and trousers, rises from the table and crosses toward the fire escape.*

AMANDA [*as he passes her*]: Son, will you do me a favor?

TOM: What?

AMANDA: Comb your hair! You look so pretty when your hair is combed!

[*Tom slouches on the sofa with the evening paper. Its enormous headline reads:* "Franco Triumphs."]

There is only one respect in which I would like you to emulate your father.

TOM: What respect is that?

AMANDA: The care he always took of his appearance. He never allowed himself to look untidy.

[*He throws down the paper and crosses to the fire escape.*]

Where are you going?

TOM: I'm going out to smoke.

AMANDA: You smoke too much. A pack a day at fifteen cents a

pack. How much would that amount to in a month? Thirty times fifteen is how much, Tom? Figure it out and you will be astounded at what you could save. Enough to give you a night-school course in accounting at Washington U.! Just think what a wonderful thing that would be for you, son!

[*Tom is unmoved by the thought.*]

TOM: I'd rather smoke. [*He steps out on the landing, letting the screen door slam.*]

AMANDA [*sharply*]: I know! That's the tragedy of it. . . . [*Alone, she turns to look at her husband's picture.*]

[*Dance music: "The World Is Waiting for the Sunrise!"*]

TOM [*to the audience*]: Across the alley from us was the Paradise Dance Hall. On evenings in spring the windows and doors were open and the music came outdoors. Sometimes the lights were turned out except for a large glass sphere that hung from the ceiling. It would turn slowly about and filter the dusk with delicate rainbow colors. Then the orchestra played a waltz or a tango, something that had a slow and sensuous rhythm. Couples would come outside, to the relative privacy of the alley. You could see them kissing behind ash pits and telephone poles. This was the compensation for lives that passed like mine, without any change or adventure. Adventure and change were imminent in this year. They were waiting around the corner for all these kids. Suspended in the mist over Berchtesgaden, caught in the folds of Chamberlain's umbrella. In Spain there was Guernica! But here there was only hot swing music and liquor, dance halls, bars, and movies, and sex that hung in the gloom like a chandelier and flooded the world with brief, deceptive rainbows. . . . All the world was waiting for bombardments!

[*Amanda turns from the picture and comes outside.*]

AMANDA [*sighing*]: A fire escape landing's a poor excuse for a porch. [*She spreads a newspaper on a step and sits down, gracefully and demurely as if she were settling into a swing on a Mississippi veranda.*] What are you looking at?

TOM: The moon.

AMANDA: Is there a moon this evening?

TOM: It's rising over Garfinkel's Delicatessen.

AMANDA: So it is! A little silver slipper of a moon. Have you made a wish on it yet?

TOM: Um-hum.

AMANDA: What did you wish for?

TOM: That's a secret.

AMANDA: A secret, huh? Well, I won't tell mine either. I will be just as mysterious as you.

TOM: I bet I can guess what yours is.

AMANDA: Is my head so transparent?

TOM: You're not a sphinx.

AMANDA: No, I don't have secrets. I'll tell you what I wished for on the moon. Success and happiness for my precious children! I wish for that whenever there's a moon, and when there isn't a moon, I wish for it, too.

TOM: I thought perhaps you wished for a gentleman caller.

AMANDA: Why do you say that?

TOM: Don't you remember asking me to fetch one?

AMANDA: I remember suggesting that it would be nice for your sister if you brought home some nice young man from the ware-house. I think that I've made that suggestion more than once.

TOM: Yes, you have made it repeatedly.

AMANDA: Well?

TOM: We are going to have one.

AMANDA: *What?*

TOM: A gentleman caller!

[*The annunciation is celebrated with music. Amanda rises. Image on screen*: A caller with a bouquet.]

AMANDA: You mean you have asked some nice young man to come over?

TOM: Yep. I've asked him to dinner.

AMANDA: You really did?

TOM: I did!

AMANDA: You did, and did he—*accept?*

TOM: He did!

AMANDA: Well, well—well, well! That's—lovely!

TOM: I thought that you would be pleased.

AMANDA: It's definite then?

TOM: Very definite.

AMANDA: Soon?

TOM: Very soon.

AMANDA: For heaven's sake, stop putting on and tell me some things, will you?

TOM: What things do you want me to tell you?

AMANDA: *Naturally* I would like to know when he's *coming!*

TOM: He's coming tomorrow.

AMANDA: *Tomorrow?*

TOM: Yep. Tomorrow.

AMANDA: But, Tom!

TOM: Yes, Mother?

AMANDA: Tomorrow gives me no time!

TOM: Time for what?

AMANDA: Preparations! Why didn't you phone me at once, as soon as you asked him, the minute that he accepted? Then, don't you see, I could have been getting ready!

TOM: You don't have to make any fuss.

AMANDA: Oh, Tom, Tom, Tom, of course I have to make a fuss! I want things nice, not sloppy! Not thrown together. I'll certainly have to do some fast thinking, won't I?

TOM: I don't see why you have to think at all.

AMANDA: You just don't know. We can't have a gentleman caller in a pigsty! All my wedding silver has to be polished, the monogrammed table linen ought to be laundered! The windows have to be washed and fresh curtains put up. And how about clothes? We have to *wear* something, don't we?

TOM: Mother, this boy is no one to make a fuss over!

AMANDA: Do you realize he's the first young man we've introduced to your sister? It's terrible, dreadful, disgraceful that poor little sister has never received a single gentleman caller! Tom, come inside! [*She opens the screen door.*]

TOM: What for?

AMANDA: I want to ask you some things.

TOM: If you're going to make such a fuss, I'll call it off, I'll tell him not to come!

AMANDA: You certainly won't do anything of the kind. Nothing offends people worse than broken engagements. It simply means I'll have to work like a Turk! We won't be brilliant, but we will pass inspection. Come on inside.

[*Tom follows her inside, groaning.*]

Sit down.

TOM: Any particular place you would like me to sit?

AMANDA: Thank heavens I've got that new sofa! I'm also making payments on a floor lamp I'll have sent out! And put the chintz covers on, they'll brighten things up! Of course I'd hoped to have these walls re-papered. . . . What is the young man's name?

TOM: His name is O'Connor.

AMANDA: That, of course, means fish—tomorrow is Friday! I'll have that salmon loaf—with Durkee's dressing! What does he do? He works at the warehouse?

TOM: Of course! How else would I—

AMANDA: Tom, he—doesn't drink?

TOM: Why do you ask me that?

AMANDA: Your father *did!*

TOM: Don't get started on that!

AMANDA: He *does* drink, then?

TOM: Not that I know of!

AMANDA: Make sure, be certain! The last thing I want for my daughter's a boy who drinks!

TOM: Aren't you being a little bit premature? Mr. O'Connor has not yet appeared on the scene!

AMANDA: But will tomorrow. To meet your sister, and what do I know about his character? Nothing! Old maids are better off than wives of drunkards!

TOM: Oh, my God!

AMANDA: Be still!

TOM [*leaning forward to whisper*]: Lots of fellows meet girls whom they don't marry!

AMANDA: Oh, talk sensibly, Tom—and don't be sarcastic! [*She has gotten a hairbrush.*]

TOM: What are you doing?

AMANDA: I'm brushing that cowlick down! [*She attacks his hair with the brush.*] What is this young man's position at the warehouse?

TOM [*submitting grimly to the brush and the interrogation*]: This young man's position is that of a shipping clerk, Mother.

AMANDA: Sounds to me like a fairly responsible job, the sort of a job *you* would be in if you just had more *get-up*. What is his salary? Have you any idea?

TOM: I would judge it to be approximately eighty-five dollars a month.

AMANDA: Well—not princely, but—

TOM: Twenty more than I make.

AMANDA: Yes, how well I know! But for a family man, eighty-five dollars a month is not much more than you can just get by on. . . .

TOM: Yes, but Mr. O'Connor is not a family man.

AMANDA: He might be, mightn't he? Some time in the future?

TOM: I see. Plans and provisions.

AMANDA: You are the only young man that I know of who ignores the fact that the future becomes the present, the present the past, and the past turns into everlasting regret if you don't plan for it!

TOM: I will think that over and see what I can make of it.

AMANDA: Don't be supercilious with your mother! Tell me some more about this—what do you call him?

TOM: James D. O'Connor. The D. is for Delaney.

AMANDA: Irish on *both* sides! *Gracious!* And doesn't drink?

TOM: Shall I call him up and ask him right this minute?

AMANDA: The only way to find out about those things is to make discreet inquiries at the proper moment. When I was a girl in Blue Mountain and it was suspected that a young man drank, the girl whose attentions he had been receiving, if any girl *was,* would sometimes speak to the minister of his church, or rather her father would if her father was living, and sort of feel him out on the young man's character. That is the way such things are discreetly handled to keep a young woman from making a tragic mistake!

TOM: Then how did you happen to make a tragic mistake?

AMANDA: That innocent look of your father's had everyone fooled! He *smiled*—the world was *enchanted!* No girl can do worse than put herself at the mercy of a handsome appearance! I hope that Mr. O'Connor is not too good-looking.

TOM: No, he's not too good-looking. He's covered with freckles and hasn't too much of a nose.

AMANDA: He's not right-down homely, though?

TOM: Not right-down homely. Just medium homely, I'd say.

AMANDA: Character's what to look for in a man.

TOM: That's what I've always said, Mother.

AMANDA: You've never said anything of the kind and I suspect you would never give it a thought.

TOM: Don't be so suspicious of me.

AMANDA: At least I hope he's the type that's up and coming.

TOM: I think he really goes in for self-improvement.

AMANDA: What reason have you to think so?

TOM: He goes to night school.

AMANDA [*beaming*]: Splendid! What does he do, I mean study?

TOM: Radio engineering and public speaking!

AMANDA: Then he has visions of being advanced in the world! Any young man who studies public speaking is aiming to have an executive job some day! And radio engineering? A thing for the future! Both of these facts are very illuminating. Those are the sort of things that a mother should know concerning any young man who comes to call on her daughter. Seriously or—not.

TOM: One little warning. He doesn't know about Laura. I didn't let on that we had dark ulterior motives. I just said, why don't you come and have dinner with us? He said okay and that was the whole conversation.

AMANDA: I bet it was! You're eloquent as an oyster. However, he'll know about Laura when he gets here. When he sees how lovely and sweet and pretty she is, he'll thank his lucky stars he was asked to dinner.

TOM: Mother, you mustn't expect too much of Laura.

AMANDA: What do you mean?

TOM: Laura seems all those things to you and me because she's ours and we love her. We don't even notice she's crippled any more.

AMANDA: Don't say crippled! You know that I never allow that word to be used!

TOM: But face facts, Mother. She is and—that's not all—

AMANDA: What do you mean "not all"?

TOM: Laura is very different from other girls.

AMANDA: I think the difference is all to her advantage.

TOM: Not quite all—in the eyes of others—strangers—she's terribly shy and lives in a world of her own and those things make her seem a little peculiar to people outside the house.

AMANDA: Don't say peculiar.

TOM: Face the facts. She is.

[*The dance hall music changes to a tango that has a minor and somewhat ominous tone.*]

AMANDA: In what way is she peculiar—may I ask?

TOM [*gently*]: She lives in a world of her own—a world of little glass ornaments, Mother. . . . [*He gets up. Amanda remains holding the brush, looking at him, troubled.*] She plays old phonograph records and—that's about all— [*He glances at himself in the mirror and crosses to the door.*]

AMANDA [*sharply*]: Where are you going?

TOM: I'm going to the movies. [*He goes out the screen door.*]

AMANDA: Not to the movies, every night to the movies! [*She follows quickly to the screen door.*] I don't believe you always go to the movies!

[*He is gone. Amanda looks worriedly after him for a moment. Then vitality and optimism return and she turns from the door, crossing to the portieres.*]

Laura! Laura!

[*Laura answers from the kitchenette.*]

LAURA: Yes, Mother.

AMANDA: Let those dishes go and come in front!

[*Laura appears with a dish towel. Amanda speaks to her gaily.*]

Laura, come here and make a wish on the moon!

[*Screen image: The Moon.*]

LAURA [*entering*]: Moon—moon?

AMANDA: A little silver slipper of a moon. Look over your left shoulder, Laura, and make a wish!

[*Laura looks faintly puzzled as if called out of sleep. Amanda seizes her shoulders and turns her at an angle by the door.*]

Now! Now, darling, *wish!*

LAURA: What shall I wish for, Mother?

AMANDA [*her voice trembling and her eyes suddenly filling with tears*]: Happiness! Good fortune!

[*The sound of the violin rises and the stage dims out.*]

SCENE SIX

The light comes up on the fire escape landing. Tom is leaning against the grill, smoking. Screen image: The high school hero.

TOM: And so the following evening I brought Jim home to dinner. I had known Jim slightly in high school. In high school Jim was a hero. He had tremendous Irish good nature and vitality with the scrubbed and polished look of white chinaware. He seemed to move in a continual spotlight. He was a star in basketball, captain of the debating club, president of the senior class and the glee club and he sang the male lead in the annual light operas. He was always running or bounding, never just walking. He seemed always at the point of defeating the law of gravity. He was shooting with such velocity through his adolescence that you would logically expect him to arrive at nothing short of the White House by the time he was thirty. But Jim apparently ran into more interference after his graduation from Soldan. His speed had definitely slowed. Six years after he left high school he was holding a job that wasn't much better than mine.

[*Screen image*: The Clerk.]

He was the only one at the warehouse with whom I was on friendly terms. I was valuable to him as someone who could remember his former glory, who had seen him win basketball games and the silver cup in debating. He knew of my secret practice of retiring to a cabinet of the washroom to work on poems when business was slack in the warehouse. He called me Shakespeare. And while the other boys in the warehouse regarded me with suspicious hostility, Jim took a humorous attitude toward me. Gradually his attitude affected the others, their hostility wore off and they also began to smile at me as people smile at an oddly fashioned dog who trots across their path at some distance.

I knew that Jim and Laura had known each other at Soldan, and I had heard Laura speak admiringly of his voice. I didn't know if Jim remembered her or not. In high school Laura had been as unobtrusive as Jim had been astonishing. If he did remember Laura, it was not as my sister, for when I asked him to dinner, he grinned and said, "You know, Shakespeare, I never thought of you as having folks!"

He was about to discover that I did. . . .

[*Legend on screen*: "The accent of a coming foot." *The light dims out on Tom and comes up in the Wingfield living room—a delicate lemony light. It is about five on a Friday evening of late spring which comes "scattering poems in the sky."*

Amanda has worked like a Turk in preparation for the gentleman caller. The results are astonishing. The new floor lamp with its rose silk shade is in place, a colored paper lantern conceals the broken light fixture in the ceiling, new billowing white curtains are at the windows, chintz covers are on the chairs and sofa, a pair of new sofa pillows make their initial appearance. Open boxes and tissue paper are scattered on the floor.

Laura stands in the middle of the room with lifted arms while Amanda crouches before her, adjusting the hem of a new dress, devout and ritualistic. The dress is colored and designed by memory. The arrangement of Laura's hair is changed; it is softer and more becoming. A fragile, unearthly prettiness has come out in Laura: she is like a piece of translucent glass touched by light, given a momentary radiance, not actual, not lasting.]

AMANDA [*impatiently*]: Why are you trembling?

LAURA: Mother, you've made me so nervous!

AMANDA: How have I made you nervous?

LAURA: By all this fuss! You make it seem so important!

AMANDA: I don't understand you, Laura. You couldn't be satisfied with just sitting home, and yet whenever I try to arrange something for you, you seem to resist it. [*She gets up.*] Now take a look at yourself. No, wait! Wait just a moment—I have an idea!

LAURA: What is it now?

[*Amanda produces two powder puffs which she wraps in handkerchiefs and stuffs in Laura's bosom.*]

LAURA: Mother, what are you doing?

AMANDA: They call them "Gay Deceivers"!

LAURA: I won't wear them!

AMANDA: You will!

LAURA: Why should I?

AMANDA: Because, to be painfully honest, your chest is flat.

LAURA: You make it seem like we were setting a trap.

AMANDA: All pretty girls are a trap, a pretty trap, and men expect them to be.

[*Legend on screen*: "A pretty trap."]

Now look at yourself, young lady. This is the prettiest you will ever be! [*She stands back to admire Laura.*] I've got to fix myself now! You're going to be surprised by your mother's appearance!

[*Amanda crosses through the portieres, humming gaily. Laura moves slowly to the long mirror and stares solemnly at herself. A wind blows the white curtains inward in a slow, graceful motion and with a faint, sorrowful sighing.*]

AMANDA [*from somewhere behind the portieres*]: It isn't dark enough yet.

[*Laura turns slowly before the mirror with a troubled look. Legend on screen*: "This is my sister: Celebrate her with strings!" *Music plays.*]

AMANDA [*laughing, still not visible*]: I'm going to show you something. I'm going to make a spectacular appearance!

LAURA: What is it, Mother?

AMANDA: Possess your soul in patience—you will see! Something I've resurrected from that old trunk! Styles haven't changed so terribly much after all. . . . [*She parts the portieres.*] Now just look at your mother! [*She wears a girlish frock of yellowed voile with a blue silk sash. She carries a bunch of jonquils—the legend of her youth is nearly revived. Now she speaks feverishly.*] This is the dress in which I led the cotillion. Won the Cakewalk twice at Sunset Hill, wore one Spring to the Governor's Ball in Jackson! See how I sashayed around the ballroom, Laura? [*She raises her skirt and does a mincing step around the room.*] I wore it on Sundays for my gentlemen callers! I had it on the day I met your father. . . . I had malaria fever all that Spring. The change of climate from East Tennessee to the Delta—weakened resistance. I had a little temperature all the time—not enough to be serious—just enough to make me restless and giddy! Invitations poured in—parties all over the Delta! "Stay in bed," said Mother, "you have a fever!"—but I just wouldn't. I took quinine but kept on going, going! Evenings, dances! Afternoons, long, long rides! Picnics—lovely! So lovely, that country in May—all lacy with dogwood, literally flooded with jonquils! That was the spring I had the craze for jonquils. Jonquils became an absolute obsession. Mother said, "Honey, there's no more room for jonquils." And still I kept on bringing in more jonquils. Whenever, wherever I saw them, I'd say, "Stop! Stop! I see jonquils!" I made the young men help me gather the jonquils! It was a joke, Amanda and her jonquils. Finally there were no more vases to hold them, every available space was filled with jonquils. No vases to hold them? All right, I'll hold them myself! And then I— [*She stops in front of the picture. Music plays.*] met your father! Malaria fever and jonquils and then—this—boy. . . . [*She switches on the rose-colored lamp.*] I hope they get here before it starts to rain. [*She crosses the room and places the jonquils in a bowl on the table.*] I gave your brother a little extra change so he and Mr. O'Connor could take the service car home.

LAURA [*with an altered look*]: What did you say his name was?

AMANDA: O'Connor.

LAURA: What is his first name?

AMANDA: I don't remember. Oh, yes, I do. It was—Jim!

[*Laura sways slightly and catches hold of a chair. Legend on screen*: "Not Jim!"]

LAURA [*faintly*]: Not—Jim!

AMANDA: Yes, that was it, it was Jim! I've never known a Jim that wasn't nice!

[*The music becomes ominous.*]

LAURA: Are you sure his name is Jim O'Connor?

AMANDA: Yes. Why?

LAURA: Is he the one that Tom used to know in high school?

AMANDA: He didn't say so. I think he just got to know him at the warehouse.

LAURA: There was a Jim O'Connor we both knew in high

school— [*Then, with effort.*] If that is the one that Tom is bringing to dinner—you'll have to excuse me, I won't come to the table.

AMANDA: What sort of nonsense is this?

LAURA: You asked me once if I'd ever liked a boy. Don't you remember I showed you this boy's picture?

AMANDA: You mean the boy you showed me in the yearbook?

LAURA: Yes, that boy.

AMANDA: Laura, Laura, were you in love with that boy?

LAURA: I don't know, Mother. All I know is I couldn't sit at the table if it was him!

AMANDA: It won't be him! It isn't the least bit likely. But whether it is or not, you will come to the table. You will not be excused.

LAURA: I'll have to be, Mother.

AMANDA: I don't intend to humor your silliness, Laura. I've had too much from you and your brother, both! So just sit down and compose yourself till they come. Tom has forgotten his key so you'll have to let them in, when they arrive.

LAURA [*panicky*]: Oh, Mother—*you* answer the door!

AMANDA [*lightly*]: I'll be in the kitchen—busy!

LAURA: Oh, Mother, please answer the door, don't make me do it!

AMANDA [*crossing into the kitchenette*]: I've got to fix the dressing for the salmon. Fuss, fuss—silliness!—over a gentleman caller!

[*The door swings shut. Laura is left alone. Legend on screen: "Terror!" She utters a low moan and turns off the lamp—sits stiffly on the edge of the sofa, knotting her fingers together.*]
    Legend on screen: "The Opening of a Door!" Tom and Jim

appear on the fire escape steps and climb to the landing. Hearing their approach, Laura rises with a panicky gesture. She retreats to the portieres. The doorbell rings. Laura catches her breath and touches her throat. Low drums sound.]

AMANDA [*calling*]: Laura, sweetheart! The door!

[*Laura stares at it without moving.*]

JIM: I think we just beat the rain.

TOM: Uh-huh. [*He rings again, nervously. Jim whistles and fishes for a cigarette.*]

AMANDA [*very, very gaily*]: Laura, that is your brother and Mr. O'Connor! Will you let them in, darling?

[*Laura crosses toward the kitchenette door.*]

LAURA [*breathlessly*]: Mother—you go to the door!

[*Amanda steps out of the kitchenette and stares furiously at Laura. She points imperiously at the door.*]

Please, please!

AMANDA [*in a fierce whisper*]: What is the matter with you, you silly thing?

LAURA [*desperately*]: Please, you answer it, *please!*

AMANDA: I told you I wasn't going to humor you, Laura. Why have you chosen this moment to lose your mind?

LAURA: Please, please, please, you go!

AMANDA: You'll have to go to the door because I can't!

LAURA [*despairingly*]: I can't either!

AMANDA: *Why?*

LAURA: I'm *sick!*

AMANDA: I'm sick, too—of your nonsense! Why can't you and your brother be normal people? Fantastic whims and behavior! [*Tom gives a long ring.*] Preposterous goings on! Can you give me one reason— [*She calls out lyrically.*] *Coming! Just one second!*— why you should be afraid to open a door? Now you answer it, Laura!

LAURA: Oh, oh, oh . . . [*She returns through the portieres, darts to the Victrola, winds it frantically and turns it on.*]

AMANDA: Laura Wingfield, you march right to that door!

LAURA: *Yes—yes, Mother!*

[*A faraway, scratchy rendition of "Dardanella" softens the air and gives her strength to move through it. She slips to the door and draws it cautiously open. Tom enters with the caller, Jim O'Connor.*]

TOM: Laura, this is Jim. Jim, this is my sister, Laura.

JIM [*stepping inside*]: I didn't know that Shakespeare had a sister!

LAURA [*retreating, stiff and trembling, from the door*]: How— how do you do?

JIM [*heartily, extending his hand*]: Okay!

[*Laura touches it hesitantly with hers.*]

JIM: Your hand's *cold*, Laura!

LAURA: Yes, well—I've been playing the Victrola. . . .

JIM: Must have been playing classical music on it! You ought to play a little hot swing music to warm you up!

LAURA: Excuse me—I haven't finished playing the Victrola. . . . [*She turns awkwardly and hurries into the front room. She pauses a second by the Victrola. Then she catches her breath and darts through the portieres like a frightened deer.*]

JIM [*grinning*]: What was the matter?

TOM: Oh—with Laura? Laura is—terribly shy.

JIM: Shy, huh? It's unusual to meet a shy girl nowadays. I don't believe you ever mentioned you had a sister.

TOM: Well, now you know. I have one. Here is the *Post Dispatch*. You want a piece of it?

JIM: Uh-huh.

TOM: What piece? The comics?

JIM: Sports! [*He glances at it.*] Ole Dizzy Dean is on his bad behavior.

TOM [*uninterested*]: Yeah? [*He lights a cigarette and goes over to the fire-escape door.*]

JIM: Where are *you* going?

TOM: I'm going out on the terrace.

JIM [*going after him*]: You know, Shakespeare—I'm going to sell you a bill of goods!

TOM: What goods?

JIM: A course I'm taking.

TOM: Huh?

JIM: In public speaking! You and me, we're not the warehouse type.

TOM: Thanks—that's good news. But what has public speaking got to do with it?

JIM: It fits you for—executive positions!

TOM: Awww.

JIM: I tell you it's done a helluva lot for me.

[*Image on screen*: Executive at his desk.]

TOM: In what respect?

JIM: In every! Ask yourself what is the difference between you an' me and men in the office down front? Brains?— No!— Ability?— No! Then what? Just one little thing—

TOM: What is that one little thing?

JIM: Primarily it amounts to—social poise! Being able to square up to people and hold your own on any social level!

AMANDA [*from the kitchenette*]: Tom?

TOM: Yes, Mother?

AMANDA: Is that you and Mr. O'Connor?

TOM: Yes, Mother.

AMANDA: Well, you just make yourselves comfortable in there.

TOM: Yes, Mother.

AMANDA: Ask Mr. O'Connor if he would like to wash his hands.

JIM: Aw, no—no—thank you—I took care of that at the warehouse. Tom—

TOM: Yes?

JIM: Mr. Mendoza was speaking to me about you.

TOM: Favorably?

JIM: What do you think?

TOM: Well—

JIM: You're going to be out of a job if you don't wake up.

TOM: I am waking up—

JIM: You show no signs.

TOM: The signs are interior.

[*Image on screen*: The sailing vessel with the Jolly Roger again.]

TOM: I'm planning to change. [*He leans over the fire escape rail, speaking with quiet exhilaration. The incandescent marquees and signs of the first-run movie houses light his face from across the alley. He looks like a voyager.*] I'm right at the point of committing myself to a future that doesn't include the warehouse and Mr. Mendoza or even a night-school course in public speaking.

JIM: What are you gassing about?

TOM: I'm tired of the movies.

JIM: Movies!

TOM: Yes, movies! Look at them— [*A wave toward the marvels of Grand Avenue.*] All of those glamorous people—having adventures—hogging it all, gobbling the whole thing up! You know what happens? People go to the *movies* instead of *moving!* Hollywood characters are supposed to have all the adventures for everybody in America, while everybody in America sits in a dark room and watches them have them! Yes, until there's a war. That's when adventure becomes available to the masses! *Everyone's* dish, not only Gable's! Then the people in the dark room come out of the dark room to have some adventures themselves—goody, goody! It's our turn now, to go to the South Sea Island—to make a safari—to be exotic, far-off! But I'm not patient. I don't want to wait till then. I'm tired of the *movies* and I am *about* to *move!*

JIM [*incredulously*]: Move?

TOM: Yes.

JIM: When?

TOM: Soon!

JIM: Where? Where?

[*The music seems to answer the question, while Tom thinks it over. He searches in his pockets.*]

TOM: I'm starting to boil inside. I know I seem dreamy, but inside—well, I'm boiling! Whenever I pick up a shoe, I shudder a little thinking how short life is and what I am doing! Whatever that means, I know it doesn't mean shoes—except as something to wear on a traveler's feet! [*He finds what be has been searching for in his pockets and holds out a paper to Jim.*] Look—

JIM: What?

TOM: I'm a member.

JIM [*reading*]: The Union of Merchant Seamen.

TOM: I paid my dues this month, instead of the light bill.

JIM: You will regret it when they turn the lights off.

TOM: I won't be here.

JIM: How about your mother?

TOM: I'm like my father. The bastard son of a bastard! Did you notice how he's grinning in his picture in there? And he's been absent going on sixteen years!

JIM: You're just talking, you drip. How does your mother feel about it?

TOM: Shhh! Here comes Mother! Mother is not acquainted with my plans!

AMANDA [*coming through the portieres*]: Where are you all?

TOM: On the terrace, Mother.

[*They start inside. She advances to them. Tom is distinctly shocked at her appearance. Even Jim blinks a little. He is making his first contact with girlish Southern vivacity and in spite of the night-school course in public speaking is somewhat thrown off the beam by the unexpected outlay of social charm. Certain responses are attempted by him but are swept aside by Amanda's gay laughter and chatter. Tom is embarrassed but after the first shock Jim reacts very warmly. He grins and chuckles, is altogether won over. Image on screen: Amanda as a girl.*]

AMANDA [*coyly smiling, shaking her girlish ringlets*]: Well, well, well, so this is Mr. O'Connor. Introductions entirely unnecessary. I've heard so much about you from my boy. I finally said to him, Tom—good gracious!—why don't you bring this paragon to supper? I'd like to meet this nice young man at the warehouse!—instead of just hearing him sing your praises so much! I don't know why my son is so stand-offish—that's not Southern behavior!

Let's sit down and—I think we could stand a little more air in here! Tom, leave the door open. I felt a nice fresh breeze a moment ago. Where has it gone to? Mmm, so warm already! And not quite summer, even. We're going to burn up when summer really gets started. However, we're having—we're having a very light supper. I think light things are better fo' this time of year. The same as light clothes are. Light clothes an' light food are what warm weather calls fo'. You know our blood gets so thick during th' winter—it takes a while fo' us to *adjust* ou'selves!—when the season changes . . . It's come so quick this year. I wasn't prepared. All of a sudden—heavens! Already summer! I ran to the trunk an' pulled out this light dress—terribly old! Historical almost! But feels so good—so good an' co-ol, y' know. . . .

TOM: Mother—

AMANDA: Yes, honey?

TOM: How about—supper?

AMANDA: Honey, you go ask Sister if supper is ready! You know that Sister is in full charge of supper! Tell her you hungry boys are waiting for it. [*To Jim.*] Have you met Laura?

JIM: She—

AMANDA: Let you in? Oh, good, you've met already! It's rare for a girl as sweet an' pretty as Laura to be domestic! But Laura is, thank heavens, not only pretty but also very domestic. I'm not at all. I never was a bit. I never could make a thing but angel-food cake. Well, in the South we had so many servants. Gone, gone, gone. All vestige of gracious living! Gone completely! I wasn't prepared for what the future brought me. All of my gentlemen callers were sons of planters and so of course I assumed that I would be married to one and raise my family on a large piece of land with plenty of servants. But man proposes—and woman accepts the proposal! To vary that old, old saying a little bit—I married no planter! I married a man who worked for the telephone company! That gallantly smiling gentleman over there! [*She points to the picture.*] A telephone man who—fell in love with long-distance! Now he travels and I don't even know where! But what am I going on for about my—tribulations? Tell me yours—I hope you don't have any! Tom?

TOM [*returning*]: Yes, Mother?

AMANDA: Is supper nearly ready?

TOM: It looks to me like supper is on the table.

AMANDA: Let me look— [*She rises prettily and looks through the portieres.*] Oh, lovely! But where is Sister?

TOM: Laura is not feeling well and she says that she thinks she'd better not come to the table.

AMANDA: What? Nonsense! Laura? Oh, Laura!

LAURA [*from the kitchenette, faintly*]: Yes, Mother.

AMANDA: You really must come to the table. We won't be seated until you come to the table! Come in, Mr. O'Connor. You sit over there, and I'll . . . Laura? Laura Wingfield! You're keeping us waiting, honey! We can't say grace until you come to the table!

[*The kitchenette door is pushed weakly open and Laura comes in. She is obviously quite faint, her lips trembling, her eyes wide and staring. She moves unsteadily toward the table. Screen legend: "Terror!" Outside a summer storm is coming on abruptly. The white curtains billow inward at the windows and there is a sorrowful murmur from the deep blue dusk. Laura suddenly stumbles; she catches at a chair with a faint moan.*]

TOM: Laura!

AMANDA: Laura!

[*There is a clap of thunder. Screenlegend: "Ah!"*]

[*Despairingly.*] Why, Laura, you *are* ill, darling! Tom, help your sister into the living room, dear! Sit in the living room, Laura—rest on the sofa. Well! [*To Jim as Tom helps his sister to the sofa in the living room.*] Standing over the hot stove made her ill! I told her that it was just too warm this evening, but—

[*Tom comes back to the table.*]

Is Laura all right now?

TOM: Yes.

AMANDA: What *is* that? Rain? A nice cool rain has come up! [*She gives Jim a frightened look.*] I think we may—have grace—now . . .

[*Tom looks at her stupidly.*] Tom, honey—you say grace!

TOM: Oh . . . "For these and all thy mercies—"

[*They bow their heads, Amanda stealing a nervous glance at Jim. In the living room Laura, stretched on the sofa, clenches her hand to her lips, to hold back a shuddering sob.*]

God's Holy Name be praised—

[*The scene dims out.*]

SCENE SEVEN

It is half an hour later. Dinner is just being finished in the dining room, Laura is still huddled upon the sofa, her feet drawn under her, her head resting on a pale blue pillow, her eyes wide and mysteriously watchful. The new floor lamp with its shade of rose-colored silk gives a soft, becoming light to her face, bringing out the fragile, unearthly prettiness which usually escapes attention. From outside there is a steady murmur of rain, but it is slackening and soon stops; the air outside becomes pale and luminous as the moon breaks through the clouds. A moment after the curtain rises, the lights in both rooms flicker and go out.

JIM: Hey, there, Mr. Light Bulb!

[*Amanda laughs nervously. Legend on screen:* "Suspension of a public service."]

AMANDA: Where was Moses when the lights went out? Ha-ha. Do you know the answer to that one, Mr. O'Connor?

JIM: No, Ma'am, what's the answer?

AMANDA: In the dark!

[*Jim laughs appreciatively.*]

Everybody sit still. I'll light the candles. Isn't it lucky we have them on the table? Where's a match? Which of you gentlemen can provide a match?

JIM: Here.

AMANDA: Thank you, Sir.

JIM: Not at all, Ma'am!

AMANDA [*as she lights the candles*]: I guess the fuse has burnt out. Mr. O'Connor, can you tell a burnt-out fuse? I know I can't and Tom is a total loss when it comes to mechanics.

[*They rise from the table and go into the kitchenette, from where their voices are heard.*]

Oh, be careful you don't bump into something. We don't want our gentleman caller to break his neck. Now wouldn't that be a fine howdy-do?

JIM: Ha-ha! Where is the fuse-box?

AMANDA: Right here next to the stove. Can you see anything?

JIM: Just a minute.

AMANDA: Isn't electricity a mysterious thing? Wasn't it Benjamin Franklin who tied a key to a kite? We live in such a mysterious universe, don't we? Some people say that science clears up all the mysteries for us. In my opinion it only creates more! Have you found it yet?

JIM: No, Ma'am. All these fuses look okay to me.

AMANDA: Tom!

TOM: Yes, Mother?

AMANDA: That light bill I gave you several days ago. The one I told you we got the notices about?

[*Legend on screen*: "Ha!"]

TOM: Oh—yeah.

AMANDA: You didn't neglect to pay it by any chance?

TOM: Why, I—

AMANDA: Didn't! I might have known it!

JIM: Shakespeare probably wrote a poem on that light bill, Mrs. Wingfield.

AMANDA: I might have known better than to trust him with it! There's such a high price for negligence in this world!

JIM: Maybe the poem will win a ten-dollar prize.

AMANDA: We'll just have to spend the remainder of the evening in the nineteenth century, before Mr. Edison made the Mazda lamp!

JIM: Candlelight is my favorite kind of light.

AMANDA: That shows you're romantic! But that's no excuse for Tom. Well, we got through dinner. Very considerate of them to let us get through dinner before they plunged us into everlasting darkness, wasn't it, Mr. O'Connor?

JIM: Ha-ha!

AMANDA: Tom, as a penalty for your carelessness you can help me with the dishes.

JIM: Let me give you a hand.

AMANDA: Indeed you will not!

JIM: I ought to be good for something.

AMANDA: Good for something? [*Her tone is rhapsodic.*] *You?* Why, Mr. O'Connor, nobody, *nobody's* given me this much entertainment in years—as you have!

JIM: Aw, now, Mrs. Wingfield!

AMANDA: I'm not exaggerating, not one bit! But Sister is all by her lonesome. You go keep her company in the parlor! I'll give you this lovely old candelabrum that used to be on the altar at the Church of the Heavenly Rest. It was melted a little out of shape when the church burnt down. Lightning struck it one spring. Gypsy Jones was holding a revival at the time and he intimated that the church was destroyed because the Episcopalians gave card parties.

JIM: Ha-ha.

AMANDA: And how about you coaxing Sister to drink a little wine? I think it would be good for her! Can you carry both at once?

JIM: Sure. I'm Superman!

AMANDA: Now, Thomas, get into this apron!

[*Jim comes into the dining room, carrying the candelabrum, its candles lighted, in one hand and a glass of wine in the other. The door of the kitchenette swings closed on Amanda's gay laughter; the flickering light approaches the portieres. Laura sits up nervously as Jim enters. She can hardly speak from the almost intolerable strain of being alone with a stranger.*

Screen legend: "I don't suppose you remember me at all!"

At first, before Jim's warmth overcomes her paralyzing shyness, Laura's voice is thin and breathless, as though she had just run up a steep flight of stairs. Jim's attitude is gently humorous. While the incident is apparently unimportant, it is to Laura the climax of her secret life.]

JIM: Hello there, Laura.

LAURA [*faintly*]: Hello. [*She clears her throat.*]

JIM: How are you feeling now? Better?

LAURA: Yes. Yes, thank you.

JIM: This is for you. A little dandelion wine. [*He extends the glass toward her with extravagant gallantry.*]

LAURA: Thank you.

JIM: Drink it—but don't get drunk! [*He laughs heartily. Laura takes the glass uncertainly; she laughs shyly.*] Where shall I set the candles?

LAURA: Oh—oh, anywhere . . .

JIM: How about here on the floor? Any objections?

LAURA: No.

JIM: I'll spread a newspaper under to catch the drippings. I like to sit on the floor. Mind if I do?

LAURA: Oh, no.

JIM: Give me a pillow?

LAURA: What?

JIM: A pillow!

LAURA: Oh . . . [*She hands him one quickly.*]

JIM: How about you? Don't you like to sit on the floor?

LAURA: Oh—yes.

JIM: Why don't you, then?

LAURA: I—will.

JIM: Take a pillow!

[*Laura does. She sits on the floor on the other side of the candelabrum. Jim crosses his legs and smiles engagingly at her.*]

I can't hardly see you sitting way over there.

LAURA: I can—see you.

JIM: I know, but that's not fair, I'm in the limelight.

[*Laura moves her pillow closer.*]

Good! Now I can see you! Comfortable?

LAURA: Yes.

JIM: So am I. Comfortable as a cow! Will you have some gum?

LAURA: No, thank you.

JIM: I think that I will indulge, with your permission. [*He musingly unwraps a stick of gum and holds it up.*] Think of the fortune made by the guy that invented the first piece of chewing gum. Amazing, huh? The Wrigley Building is one of the sights of Chicago—I saw it when I went up to the Century of Progress. Did you take in the Century of Progress?

LAURA: No, I didn't.

JIM: Well, it was quite a wonderful exposition. What impressed me most was the Hall of Science. Gives you an idea of what the future will be in America, even more wonderful than the present time is! [*There is a pause. Jim smiles at her.*] Your brother tells me you're shy. Is that right, Laura?

LAURA: I—don't know.

JIM: I judge you to be an old-fashioned type of girl. Well, I think that's a pretty good type to be. Hope you don't think I'm being too personal—do you?

LAURA: [*hastily, out of embarrassment*]: I believe I *will* take a piece of gum, if you—don't mind. [*Clearing her throat.*] Mr. O'Connor, have you—kept up with your singing?

JIM: Singing? Me?

LAURA: Yes. I remember what a beautiful voice you had.

JIM: When did you hear me sing?

[*Laura does not answer, and in the long pause which follows a man's voice is heard singing offstage.*]

VOICE:

O blow, ye winds, heigh-ho,
A-roving I will go!
I'm off to my love
With a boxing glove—
Ten thousand miles away!

JIM: You say you've heard me sing?

LAURA: Oh, yes! Yes, very often . . . I—don't suppose—you remember me—at all?

JIM [*smiling doubtfully*]: You know I have an idea I've seen you before. I had that idea soon as you opened the door. It seemed almost like I was about to remember your name. But the name that I started to call you—wasn't a name! And so I stopped myself before I said it.

LAURA: Wasn't it—Blue Roses?

JIM [*springing up, grinning*]: Blue Roses! My gosh, yes—Blue Roses! That's what I had on my tongue when you opened the door! Isn't it funny what tricks your memory plays? I didn't connect you with high school somehow or other. But that's where it was; it was high school. I didn't even know you were Shakespeare's sister! Gosh, I'm sorry.

LAURA: I didn't expect you to. You—barely knew me!

JIM: But we did have a speaking acquaintance, huh?

LAURA: Yes, we—spoke to each other.

JIM: When did you recognize me?

LAURA: Oh, right away!

JIM: Soon as I came in the door?

LAURA: When I heard your name I thought it was probably you. I knew that Tom used to know you a little in high school. So when you came in the door—well, then I was—sure.

JIM: Why didn't you *say* something, then?

LAURA [*breathlessly*]: I didn't know what to say, I was—too surprised!

JIM: For goodness' sakes! You know, this sure is funny!

LAURA: Yes! Yes, isn't it, though . . .

JIM: Didn't we have a class in something together?

LAURA: Yes, we did.

JIM: What class was that?

LAURA: It was—singing—chorus!

JIM: Aw!

LAURA: I sat across the aisle from you in the auditorium.

JIM: Aw.

LAURA: Mondays, Wednesdays, and Fridays.

JIM: Now I remember—you always came in late.

LAURA: Yes, it was so hard for me, getting upstairs. I had that brace on my leg—it clumped so loud!

JIM: I never heard any clumping.

LAURA [*wincing at the recollection*]: To me it sounded like—thunder!

JIM: Well, well, well, I never even noticed.

LAURA: And everybody was seated before I came in. I had to walk in front of all those people. My seat was in the back row. I had to go clumping all the way up the aisle with everyone watching!

JIM: You shouldn't have been self-conscious.

LAURA: I know, but I was. It was always such a relief when the singing started.

JIM: Aw, yes, I've placed you now! I used to call you Blue Roses. How was it that I got started calling you that?

LAURA: I was out of school a little while with pleurosis. When I came back you asked me what was the matter. I said I had pleurosis—you thought I said *Blue Roses.* That's what you always called me after that!

JIM: I hope you didn't mind.

LAURA: Oh, no—I liked it. You see, I wasn't acquainted with many—people. . . .

JIM: As I remember you sort of stuck by yourself.

LAURA: I—I—never have had much luck at—making friends.

JIM: I don't see why you wouldn't.

LAURA: Well, I—started out badly.

JIM: You mean being—

LAURA: Yes, it sort of—stood between me—

JIM: You shouldn't have let it!

LAURA: I know, but it did, and—

JIM: You were shy with people!

LAURA: I tried not to be but never could—

JIM: Overcome it?

LAURA: No, I—I never could!

JIM: I guess being shy is something you have to work out of kind of gradually.

LAURA [*sorrowfully*]: Yes—I guess it—

JIM: Takes time!

LAURA: Yes—

JIM: People are not so dreadful when you know them. That's what you have to remember! And everybody has problems, not just you, but practically everybody has got some problems. You think of yourself as having the only problems, as being the only one who is disappointed. But just look around you and you will see lots of people as disappointed as you are. For instance, I hoped when I was going to high school that I would be further along at this time, six years later, than I am now. You remember that wonderful write-up I had in *The Torch?*

LAURA: Yes! [*She rises and crosses to the table.*]

JIM: It said I was bound to succeed in anything I went into!

[*Laura returns with the high school yearbook.*]

Holy Jeez! *The Torch!*

[*He accepts it reverently. They smile across the book with mutual wonder. Laura crouches beside him and they begin to turn the pages. Laura's shyness is dissolving in his warmth.*]

LAURA: Here you are in *The Pirates of Penzance!*

JIM [*wistfully*]: I sang the baritone lead in that operetta.

LAURA [*raptly*]: So—*beautifully!*

JIM [*protesting*]: Aw—

LAURA: Yes, yes—beautifully—beautifully!

JIM: You heard me?

LAURA: All three times!

JIM: No!

LAURA: Yes!

JIM: All three performances?

LAURA [*looking down*]: Yes.

JIM: Why?

LAURA: I—wanted to ask you to—autograph my program. [*She takes the program from the back of the yearbook and shows it to him.*]

JIM: Why didn't you ask me to?

LAURA: You were always surrounded by your own friends so much that I never had a chance to.

JIM: You should have just—

LAURA: Well, I—thought you might think I was—

JIM: Thought I might think you was—what?

LAURA: Oh—

JIM [*with reflective relish*]: I was beleaguered by females in those days.

LAURA: You were terribly popular!

JIM: Yeah—

LAURA: You had such a—friendly way—

JIM: I was spoiled in high school.

LAURA: Everybody—liked you!

JIM: Including you?

LAURA: I—yes, I—did, too— [*She gently closes the book in her lap.*]

JIM: Well, well, well! Give me that program, Laura. [*She hands it to him. He signs it with a flourish.*] There you are—better late than never!

LAURA: Oh, I—what a—surprise!

JIM: My signature isn't worth very much right now. But some day—maybe—it will increase in value! Being disappointed is one thing and being discouraged is something else. I am disappointed but I am not discouraged. I'm twenty-three years old. How old are you?

LAURA: I'll be twenty-four in June.

JIM: That's not old age!

LAURA: No, but—

JIM: You finished high school?

LAURA [*with difficulty*]: I didn't go back.

JIM: You mean you dropped out?

LAURA: I made bad grades in my final examinations. [*She rises and replaces the book and the program on the table. Her voice is strained.*] How is—Emily Meisenbach getting along?

JIM: Oh, that kraut-head!

LAURA: Why do you call her that?

JIM: That's what she was.

LAURA: You're not still—going with her?

JIM: I never see her.

LAURA: It said in the "Personal" section that you were—engaged!

JIM: I know, but I wasn't impressed by that—propaganda!

LAURA: It wasn't—the truth?

JIM: Only in Emily's optimistic opinion!

LAURA: Oh—

[*Legend*: "What have you done since high school?"
   Jim lights a cigarette and leans indolently back on his elbows smiling at Laura with a warmth and charm which lights her inwardly with altar candles. She remains by the table, picks up a piece from the glass menagerie collection, and turns it in her hands to cover her tumult.]

JIM [*after several reflective puffs on his cigarette*]: What have you done since high school?

[*She seems not to hear him.*]

Huh?

[*Laura looks up.*]

I said what have you done since high school, Laura?

LAURA: Nothing much.

JIM: You must have been doing something these six long years.

LAURA: Yes.

JIM: Well, then, such as what?

LAURA: I took a business course at business college—

JIM: How did that work out?

LAURA: Well, not very—well—I had to drop out, it gave me— indigestion—

[*Jim laughs gently.*]

JIM: What are you doing now?

LAURA: I don't do anything—much. Oh, please don't think I sit around doing nothing! My glass collection takes up a good deal of time. Glass is something you have to take good care of.

JIM: What did you say—about glass?

LAURA: Collection I said—I have one— [*She clears her throat and turns away again, acutely shy.*]

JIM [*abruptly*]: You know what I judge to be the trouble with you? Inferiority complex! Know what that is? That's what they call it when someone low-rates himself! I understand it because I had it, too. Although my case was not so aggravated as yours seems to be. I had it until I took up public speaking, developed my voice, and learned that I had an aptitude for science. Before that time I never thought of myself as being outstanding in any way whatsoever! Now I've never made a regular study of it, but I have a friend who says I can analyze people better than doctors that make a profession of it. I don't claim that to be necessarily true, but I can sure guess a person's psychology, Laura! [*He takes out his gum.*] Excuse me, Laura. I always take it out when the flavor is gone. I'll use this scrap of paper to wrap it in. I know how it is to get it stuck on a shoe. [*He wraps the gum in paper and puts it in his pocket.*] Yep—that's what I judge to be your principal trouble. A lack of confidence in yourself as a person. You don't have the proper amount of faith in yourself. I'm basing that fact on a number of your remarks and also on certain observations I've made. For instance that clumping you thought was so awful in high school. You say that you even dreaded to walk into class. You see what you did? You dropped out of school, you gave up an education because of a clump, which as far as I know was practically non-existent! A little physical defect is what you have. Hardly noticeable even! Magnified thousands of times by imagination! You know what my strong advice to you is? Think of yourself as *superior* in some way!

LAURA: In what way would I think?

JIM: Why, man alive, Laura! Just look about you a little. What do you see? A world full of common people! All of 'em born and all of 'em going to die! Which of them has one-tenth of your good points! Or mine! Or anyone else's, as far as that goes—gosh! Everybody excels in some one thing. Some in many! [*He unconsciously glances at himself in the mirror.*] All you've got to do is discover in *what!* Take me, for instance. [*He adjusts his tie at the mirror.*] My interest happens to lie in electro-dynamics. I'm taking a course in radio engineering at night school, Laura, on top of a fairly responsible job at the warehouse. I'm taking that course and studying public speaking.

LAURA: Ohhhh.

JIM: Because I believe in the future of television! [*Turning his back to her.*] I wish to be ready to go up right along with it. Therefore I'm planning to get in on the ground floor. In fact I've already made the right connections and all that remains is for the industry itself to get under way! Full steam— [*His eyes are starry.*] *Knowledge*—Zzzzzp! *Money*—Zzzzzzp!—*Power!* That's the cycle democracy is built on! [*His attitude is convincingly dynamic. Laura stares at him, even her shyness eclipsed in her absolute wonder. He suddenly grins.*] I guess you think I think a lot of myself!

LAURA: No—o-o-o, I—

JIM: Now how about you? Isn't there something you take more interest in than anything else?

LAURA: Well, I do—as I said—have my—glass collection—

[*A peal of girlish laughter rings from the kitchenette.*]

JIM: I'm not right sure I know what you're talking about. What kind of glass is it?

LAURA: Little articles of it, they're ornaments mostly! Most of them are little animals made out of glass, the tiniest little animals in the world. Mother calls them a glass menagerie! Here's an example of one, if you'd like to see it! This one is one of the oldest. It's nearly thirteen.

[*Music: "The Glass Menagerie." He stretches out his hand.*]

Oh, be careful—if you breathe, it breaks!

JIM: I'd better not take it. I'm pretty clumsy with things.

LAURA: Go on, I trust you with him! [*She places the piece in his palm.*] There now—you're holding him gently! Hold him over the light, he loves the light! You see how the light shines through him?

JIM: It sure does shine!

LAURA: I shouldn't be partial, but he is my favorite one.

JIM: What kind of a thing is this one supposed to be?

LAURA: Haven't you noticed the single horn on his forehead?

JIM: A unicorn, huh?

LAURA: Mmmm-hmmm!

JIM: Unicorns—aren't they extinct in the modern world?

LAURA: I know!

JIM: Poor little fellow, he must feel sort of lonesome.

LAURA [*smiling*]: Well, if he does, he doesn't complain about it. He stays on a shelf with some horses that don't have horns and all of them seem to get along nicely together.

JIM: How do you know?

LAURA [*lightly*]: I haven't heard any arguments among them!

JIM [*grinning*]: No arguments, huh? Well, that's a pretty good sign! Where shall I set him?

LAURA: Put him on the table. They all like a change of scenery once in a while!

JIM: Well, well, well, well— [*He places the glass piece on the table, then raises his arms and stretches.*] Look how big my shadow is when I stretch!

LAURA: Oh, oh, yes—it stretches across the ceiling!

JIM [*crossing to the door*]: I think it's stopped raining. [*He opens the fire-escape door and the background music changes to a dance tune.*] Where does the music come from?

LAURA: From the Paradise Dance Hall across the alley.

JIM: How about cutting the rug a little, Miss Wingfield?

LAURA: Oh, I—

JIM: Or is your program filled up? Let me have a look at it. [*He grasps an imaginary card.*] Why, every dance is taken! I'll just have to scratch some out.

[*Waltz music*: "*La Golondrina.*"]

Ahhh, a waltz! [*He executes some sweeping turns by himself, then holds his arms toward Laura.*]

LAURA [*breathlessly*]: I—can't dance!

JIM: There you go, that inferiority stuff!

LAURA: I've never danced in my life!

JIM: Come on, try!

LAURA: Oh, but I'd step on you!

JIM: I'm not made out of glass.

LAURA: How—how—how do we start?

JIM: Just leave it to me. You hold your arms out a little.

LAURA: Like this?

JIM [*taking her in his arms*]: A little bit higher. Right. Now don't tighten up, that's the main thing about it—relax.

LAURA [*laughing breathlessly*]: It's hard not to.

JIM: Okay.

LAURA: I'm afraid you can't budge me.

JIM: What do you bet I can't? [*He swings her into motion.*]

LAURA: Goodness, yes, you can!

JIM: Let yourself go, now, Laura, just let yourself go.

LAURA: I'm—

JIM: Come on!

LAURA: —trying!

JIM: Not so stiff—easy does it!

LAURA: I know but I'm—

JIM: Loosen th' backbone! There now, that's a lot better.

LAURA: Am I?

JIM: Lots, lots better! [*He moves her about the room in a clumsy waltz.*]

LAURA: Oh, my!

JIM: Ha-ha!

LAURA: Oh, my goodness!

JIM: Ha-ha-ha!

[*They suddenly bump into the table, and the glass piece on it falls to the floor. Jim stops the dance.*]

What did we hit on?

LAURA: Table.

JIM: Did something fall off it? I think—

LAURA: Yes.

JIM: I hope that it wasn't the little glass horse with the horn!

LAURA: Yes. [*She stoops to pick it up.*]

JIM: Aw, aw, aw. Is it broken?

LAURA: Now it is just like all the other horses.

JIM: It's lost its—

LAURA: Horn! It doesn't matter. Maybe it's a blessing in disguise.

JIM: You'll never forgive me. I bet that that was your favorite piece of glass.

LAURA: I don't have favorites much. It's no tragedy, Freckles. Glass breaks so easily. No matter how careful you are. The traffic jars the shelves and things fall off them.

JIM: Still I'm awfully sorry that I was the cause.

LAURA [*smiling*]: I'll just imagine he had an operation. The horn was removed to make him feel less—freakish! [*They both laugh.*] Now he will feel more at home with the other horses, the ones that don't have horns. . . .

JIM: Ha-ha, that's very funny! [*Suddenly he is serious.*] I'm glad to see that you have a sense of humor. You know—you're—well—very different! Surprisingly different from anyone else I know! [*His voice becomes soft and hesitant with a genuine feeling.*] Do you mind me telling you that?

[*Laura is abashed beyond speech.*]

I mean it in a nice way—

[*Laura nods shyly, looking away.*]

JIM: You make me feel sort of—I don't know how to put it! I'm usually pretty good at expressing things, but—this is something that I don't know how to say!

[*Laura touches her throat and clears it—turns the broken unicorn in her hands. His voice becomes softer.*]

Has anyone ever told you that you were pretty?

[*There is a pause, and the music rises slightly. Laura looks up slowly, with wonder, and shakes her head.*]

Well, you are! In a very different way from anyone else. And all the nicer because of the difference, too.

[*His voice becomes low and husky. Laura turns away, nearly faint with the novelty of her emotions.*]

I wish that you were my sister. I'd teach you to have some confidence in yourself. The different people are not like other people, but being different is nothing to be ashamed of. Because other people are not such wonderful people. They're one hundred times one thousand. You're one times one! They walk all over the earth. You just stay here. They're common as—weeds, but—you—well, you're—*Blue Roses!*

[*Image on screen*: Blue Roses. *The music changes.*]

LAURA: But blue is wrong for—roses. . . .

JIM: It's right for you! You're—pretty!

LAURA: In what respect am I pretty?

JIM: In all respects—believe me! Your eyes—your hair—are pretty! Your hands are pretty! [*He catches hold of her hand.*] You think I'm making this up because I'm invited to dinner and have to be nice. Oh, I could do that! I could put on an act for you, Laura, and say lots of things without being very sincere. But this time I am. I'm talking to you sincerely. I happened to notice you had this inferiority complex that keeps you from feeling comfortable with people. Somebody needs to build your confidence up and make you proud instead of shy and turning away and—blushing. Somebody—ought to—*kiss* you, Laura!

[*His hand slips slowly up her arm to her shoulder as the music swells tumultuously. He suddenly turns her about and kisses her on the lips. When he releases her, Laura sinks on the sofa with a bright, dazed look. Jim backs away and fishes in his pocket for a cigarette. Legend on screen:* "A souvenir."]

Stumblejohn!

[*He lights the cigarette, avoiding her look. There is a peal of girlish laughter from Amanda in the kitchenette. Laura slowly raises and opens her hand. It still contains the little broken glass animal. She looks at it with a tender, bewildered expression.*]

Stumblejohn! I shouldn't have done that—that was way off the beam. You don't smoke, do you?

[*She looks up, smiling, not hearing the question. He sits beside her rather gingerly. She looks at him speechlessly—waiting. He coughs decorously and moves a little farther aside as he considers the situation and senses her feelings, dimly, with perturbation. He speaks gently.*]

Would you—care for a—mint?

[*She doesn't seem to hear him but her look grows brighter even.*]

Peppermint? Life Saver? My pocket's a regular drugstore—wherever I go. . . . [*He pops a mint in his mouth. Then he gulps and decides to make a clean breast of it. He speaks slowly and gingerly.*] Laura, you know, if I had a sister like you, I'd do the same thing as Tom. I'd bring out fellows and—introduce her to them. The right type of boys—of a type to—appreciate her. Only—well—he made a mistake about me. Maybe I've got no call to be saying this. That may not have been the idea in having me over. But what if it was? There's nothing wrong about that. The only trouble is that in my case—I'm not in a situation to—do the right thing. I can't take down your number and say I'll phone. I can't call up next week and—ask for a date. I thought I had better explain the situation in case you—misunderstood it and—I hurt your feelings. . . .

[*There is a pause. Slowly, very slowly, Laura's look changes, her eyes returning slowly from his to the glass figure in her palm. Amanda utters another gay laugh in the kitchenette.*]

LAURA [*faintly*]: You—won't—call again?

JIM: No, Laura, I can't. [*He rises from the sofa.*] As I was just explaining, I've—got strings on me. Laura, I've—been going steady! I go out all the time with a girl named Betty. She's a home-girl like you, and Catholic, and Irish, and in a great many ways we—get along fine. I met her last summer on a moonlight boat trip up the river to Alton, on the *Majestic*. Well—right away from the start it was—love!

[*Legend: "Love!" Laura sways slightly forward and grips the arm of the sofa. He fails to notice, now enrapt in his own comfortable being.*]

Being in love has made a new man of me!

[*Leaning stiffly forward, clutching the arm of the sofa, Laura struggles visibly with her storm. But Jim is oblivious; she is a long way off.*]

The power of love is really pretty tremendous! Love is something that—changes the whole world, Laura!

[*The storm abates a little and Laura leans back. He notices her again.*]

It happened that Betty's aunt took sick, she got a wire and had to go to Centralia. So Tom—when he asked me to dinner—I naturally just accepted the invitation, not knowing that you—that he—that I— [*He stops awkwardly.*] Huh—I'm a stumblejohn!

[*He flops back on the sofa. The holy candles on the altar of Laura's face have been snuffed out. There is a look of almost infinite desolation. Jim glances at her uneasily.*]

I wish that you would—say something.

[*She bites her lip which was trembling and then bravely smiles. She opens her hand again on the broken glass figure. Then she*]

gently takes his hand and raises it level with her own. She care-
fully places the unicorn in the palm of his hand, then pushes his
fingers closed upon it.]

What are you—doing that for? You want me to have him? Laura?

[*She nods.*]

What for?

LAURA: A—souvenir. . . .

[*She rises unsteadily and crouches beside the Victrola to wind*
it up. Legend on screen: "Things have a way of turning out so
badly!" *Or image:* Gentleman caller waving goodbye—gaily.

At this moment Amanda rushes brightly back into the living
room. She bears a pitcher of fruit punch in an old-fashioned
cut-glass pitcher, and a plate of macaroons. The plate has a gold
border and poppies painted on it.]

AMANDA: Well, well, well! Isn't the air delightful after the
shower? I've made you children a little liquid refreshment. [*She*
turns gaily to Jim.] Jim, do you know that song about lemonade?

> "Lemonade, lemonade
> Made in the shade and stirred with a spade—
> Good enough for any old maid!"

JIM [*uneasily*]: Ha-ha! No—I never heard it.

AMANDA: Why, Laura! You look so serious!

JIM: We were having a serious conversation.

AMANDA: Good! Now you're better acquainted!

JIM [*uncertainly*]: Ha-ha! Yes.

AMANDA: You modern young people are much more serious-
minded than my generation. I was so gay as a girl!

JIM: You haven't changed, Mrs. Wingfield.

AMANDA: Tonight I'm rejuvenated! The gaiety of the occasion, Mr. O'Connor! [*She tosses her head with a peal of laughter, spilling some lemonade.*] Oooo! I'm baptizing myself!

JIM: Here—let me—

AMANDA [*setting the pitcher down*]: There now. I discovered we had some maraschino cherries. I dumped them in, juice and all!

JIM: You shouldn't have gone to that trouble, Mrs. Wingfield.

AMANDA: Trouble, trouble? Why, it was loads of fun! Didn't you hear me cutting up in the kitchen? I bet your ears were burning! I told Tom how outdone with him I was for keeping you to himself so long a time! He should have brought you over much, much sooner! Well, now that you've found your way, I want you to be a very frequent caller! Not just occasional but all the time. Oh, we're going to have a lot of gay times together! I see them coming! Mmm, just breathe that air! So fresh, and the moon's so pretty! I'll skip back out—I know where my place is when young folks are having a—serious conversation!

JIM: Oh, don't go out, Mrs. Wingfield. The fact of the matter is I've got to be going.

AMANDA: Going, now? You're joking! Why, it's only the shank of the evening, Mr. O'Connor!

JIM: Well, you know how it is.

AMANDA: You mean you're a young workingman and have to keep workingmen's hours. We'll let you off early tonight. But only on the condition that next time you stay later. What's the best night for you? Isn't Saturday night the best night for you workingmen?

JIM: I have a couple of time-clocks to punch, Mrs. Wingfield. One at morning, another one at night!

AMANDA: My, but you *are* ambitious! You work at night, too?

JIM: No, Ma'am, not work but—Betty!

[*He crosses deliberately to pick up his hat. The band at the Paradise Dance Hall goes into a tender waltz.*]

AMANDA: Betty? Betty? Who's—Betty!

[*There is an ominous cracking sound in the sky.*]

JIM: Oh, just a girl. The girl I go steady with!

[*He smiles charmingly. The sky falls. Legend: "The Sky Falls."*]

AMANDA [*a long-drawn exhalation*]: Ohhhh . . . Is it a serious romance, Mr. O'Connor?

JIM: We're going to be married the second Sunday in June.

AMANDA: Ohhhh—how nice! Tom didn't mention that you were engaged to be married.

JIM: The cat's not out of the bag at the warehouse yet. You know how they are. They call you Romeo and stuff like that. [*He stops at the oval mirror to put on his hat. He carefully shapes the brim and the crown to give a discreetly dashing effect.*] It's been a wonderful evening, Mrs. Wingfield. I guess this is what they mean by Southern hospitality.

AMANDA: It really wasn't anything at all.

JIM: I hope it don't seem like I'm rushing off. But I promised Betty I'd pick her up at the Wabash depot, an' by the time I get my jalopy down there her train'll be in. Some women are pretty upset if you keep 'em waiting.

AMANDA: Yes, I know—the tyranny of women! [*She extends her hand.*] Goodbye, Mr. O'Connor. I wish you luck—and happiness—and success! All three of them, and so does Laura! Don't you, Laura?

LAURA: Yes!

JIM [*taking Laura's hand*]: Goodbye, Laura. I'm certainly going to treasure that souvenir. And don't you forget the good advice I gave you. [*He raises his voice to a cheery shout.*] So long, Shakespeare! Thanks again, ladies. Good night!

[*He grins and ducks jauntily out. Still bravely grimacing, Amanda closes the door on the gentleman caller. Then she turns back to the room with a puzzled expression. She and Laura don't dare to face each other. Laura crouches beside the Victrola to wind it.*]

AMANDA [*faintly*]: Things have a way of turning out so badly. I don't believe that I would play the Victrola. Well, well—well! Our gentleman caller was engaged to be married! [*She raises her voice.*] Tom!

TOM [*from the kitchenette*]: Yes, Mother?

AMANDA: Come in here a minute. I want to tell you something awfully funny.

TOM [*entering with a macaroon and a glass of the lemonade*]: Has the gentleman caller gotten away already?

AMANDA: The gentleman caller has made an early departure. What a wonderful joke you played on us!

TOM: How do you mean?

AMANDA: You didn't mention that he was engaged to be married.

TOM: Jim? Engaged?

AMANDA: That's what he just informed us.

TOM: I'll be jiggered! I didn't know about that.

AMANDA: That seems very peculiar.

TOM: What's peculiar about it?

AMANDA: Didn't you call him your best friend down at the warehouse?

TOM: He is, but how did I know?

AMANDA: It seems extremely peculiar that you wouldn't know your best friend was going to be married!

TOM: The warehouse is where I work, not where I know things about people!

AMANDA: You don't know things anywhere! You live in a dream; you manufacture illusions!

[*He crosses to the door.*]

Where are you going?

TOM: I'm going to the movies.

AMANDA: That's right, now that you've had us make such fools of ourselves. The effort, the preparations, all the expense! The new floor lamp, the rug, the clothes for Laura! All for what? To entertain some other girl's fiancé! Go to the movies, go! Don't think about us, a mother deserted, an unmarried sister who's crippled and has no job! Don't let anything interfere with your selfish pleasure! Just go, go, go—to the movies!

TOM: All right, I will! The more you shout about my selfishness to me the quicker I'll go, and I won't go to the movies!

AMANDA: Go, then! Go to the moon—you selfish dreamer!

[*Tom smashes his glass on the floor. He plunges out on the fire escape, slamming the door. Laura screams in fright. The dance-hall music becomes louder. Tom stands on the fire escape, gripping the rail. The moon breaks through the storm clouds, illuminating his face.*

Legend on screen: "And so goodbye . . ."

Tom's closing speech is timed with what is happening inside the house. We see, as though through soundproof glass, that Amanda appears to be making a comforting speech to Laura, who is huddled upon the sofa. Now that we cannot hear the mother's speech, her silliness is gone and she has dignity and tragic beauty. Laura's hair hides her face until, at the end of the speech, she lifts her head to smile at her mother. Amanda's gestures are slow and graceful, almost dancelike, as she comforts her daughter. At the end of her speech she glances a moment at the father's picture—then withdraws through the portieres. At the close of Tom's speech, Laura blows out the candles, ending the play.]

TOM: I didn't go to the moon, I went much further—for time is the longest distance between two places. Not long after that I was fired for writing a poem on the lid of a shoe-box. I left Saint Louis. I descended the steps of this fire escape for a last time and followed, from then on, in my father's footsteps, attempting to find in motion what was lost in space. I traveled around a great deal. The cities swept about me like dead leaves, leaves that were brightly colored but torn away from the branches. I would have stopped, but I was pursued by something. It always came upon me unawares, taking me altogether by surprise. Perhaps it was a familiar bit of music. Perhaps it was only a piece of transparent glass. Perhaps I am walking along a street at night, in some strange city, before I have found companions. I pass the lighted window of a shop where perfume is sold. The window is filled with pieces of colored glass, tiny transparent bottles in delicate colors, like bits of a shattered rainbow. Then all at once my sister touches my shoulder. I turn around and look into her eyes. Oh, Laura, Laura, I tried to leave you behind me, but I am more faithful than I intended to be! I reach for a cigarette, I cross the street, I run into the movies or a bar, I buy a drink, I speak to the nearest stranger—anything that can blow your candles out!

[*Laura bends over the candles.*]

For nowadays the world is lit by lightning! Blow out your candles, Laura—and so goodbye. . . .

[*She blows the candles out.*]

OPENING NIGHT REVIEWS

"Great Actress Proves It In Fine Play"
by Ashton Stevens
The Chicago Herald American, December 27, 1944

It would be very easy to say that in last evening's premiere of Tennessee Williams' *The Glass Menagerie,* at the Civic Theater, Laurette Taylor submitted as distinguished an achievement in acting as has been offered to American playgoers since Eleanora Duse gave them her last performances on this planet. So why not say it? As the burbling, down-at-the-heel mother of Eddie Dowling's worker and dreamer in a warehouse, and Julie Haydon's shy, lovelorn, and crippled moonbeam of a daughter, Miss Taylor, in a role which might have been named Fallen Grandeur, reached the peak of a theatrical career that, despite interruptions and indolences, has been going only upward for as much of the current century as has been crossed off the calendar.

In a beautiful and mystically vivid play, whose setting and lighting by Jo Mielziner is a new note in the poetics of the modern stagery, Laurette Taylor vouchsafes a characterization that is more than beautiful. It removed this first-nighter so far from this earth that the return to mundane desk and typewriter finds him unaccustomedly dizzy in the head, to say nothing of the heart. Fifty years of first-nighting have provided him with very few jolts so miraculously electrical as the jolt Laurette Taylor gave him last night.

Whether Mr. Williams' play is as undebatably great as Miss Taylor's performance, I have my just doubts. But it is a lovely thing, and an original thing. It has the courage of true poetry couched in colloquial prose. It is eerie and earthy in the same breath. It is never glossy and glittering and Broadwise. Its unforced wit is as pure as its understated pathos. It glows most humanly in a sustained atmosphere of other-worldliness.

How much of it is symbolism I do not know, nor seem to care to know. You might call it a series of dramatic sketches, each one prefaced, as was the Moscow Art Theater's *The Brothers Karamazov,* by an always enlightening and sometimes ironical narrator. Only here the narrator is also one of the principal characters—in fact, Mr. Dowling, who not only acts the youthful, restless visionary son as no lad of half his years could hope to act him, but has directed (together with Margo Jones) the presentation with a sensitiveness and appreciation such as perhaps only the author fully realizes.

Sometimes hidden, sometimes revealed, is the love story of the crippled daughter, superbly played by Miss Haydon. It comes to realization when her brother brings home from the warehouse the gusty rough fellow his sister had secretly loved at school. Anthony Ross gives him lusty identity. He is—to go back a quarter of a century for the name—a budding Babbitt, but with a friendliness as contagious as his self-confidence. He cheers the girl, breaks her painful silences, dances her to the old Victrola records her deserter father left behind, even kisses her.

But his is not the kind of kiss on which romantic curtains commonly crash. He has his own girl, and they are to be June-married; and so he won't come back to this ghostly little alley flat in St. Louis.

And the brother goes, and he won't be back to the little flat, either, but will follow the vagrant footsteps of his long-departed father, who is one of the most telling characters in the play, although all you see of him is the beaming photograph he left behind.

That's about all there is. There isn't, as Miss Barrymore and her hundred imitators used to say, any more. The burbling mother with her gorgeous imaginotions of southern aristocracy (albeit she married a telephone wireman instead of a cotton planter) and her crippled daughter with her treasured menagerie of miniature glass animals are left there alone, as Life sometime does leave women, and the Stage hardly ever.

The play leaves you in the air. But I like this air. It is rare, rich.

It is the only air in which a woman so powerfully enchanting as Laurette Taylor's Mother could have her being.

P.S.—From neighboring seats I heard William Saroyan mentioned, and Paul Vincent Carroll, and Sean O'Casey, and even a playwright named Barrie. But the only author's name I could think of was Tennessee Williams, whose magic is all his own.

"Fragile Drama Holds Theater in Tight Spell"
by Claudia Cassidy
Chicago Tribune, December 27, 1944

Too many theatrical bubbles burst in the blowing, but "The Glass Menagerie" holds in its shadowed fragility the stamina of success. This brand new play, which turned the Civic theater into a place of steadily increasing enchantment last night, is still fluid with change, but it is vividly written, and in the main superbly acted. Paradoxically, it is a dream in the dusk and a tough little play that knows people and how they tick. Etched in the shadows of a man's memory, it comes alive in theater terms of words, motion, lighting, and music. If it is your play, as it is mine, it reaches out tentacles, first tentative, then gripping, and you are caught in its spell.

Tennessee Williams, who wrote it, has been unbelievably lucky. His play, which might have been smashed by the insensitive or botched by the fatuous, has fallen into expert hands. He found Eddie Dowling, who liked it enough to fight for it, Jo Mielziner, who devoted his first time out of army service to lighting it magnificently, and Laurette Taylor, who chose it for her return to the stage. He found other people, too, but ah, that Laurette Taylor!

I never saw Miss Taylor as Peg [in Hartley Manners's 1912 play *Peg o' My Heart*], but if that was the role of her youth, this is the role of her maturity. As a draggled southern belle who married the wrong man, living in a near-tenement, alienating her children by her nagging fight to shove them up to her pathetically remembered gentility, she gives a magnificent performance. The crest of her career in the delta was the simultaneous arrival of 17 gentlemen callers, and her pitiful quest in this play—as often funny as sad—is the acquisition of just one gentleman caller for her neurotically shy daughter, the crippled girl played by Julie Haydon. Her preparations for that creature, once she has heckled her son into inviting him, his arrival in the hilarious extrovert played by Anthony Ross, and the aftermath of frustration—these are not things quckly told in their true terms. They are theater, and they take seeing.

Fortunately, I have been able to hang around the Civic at previews and I have seen "The Glass Menagerie" twice. Mr. Dowling was good last night in the double role of the son and narrator (who says the first narrator was the angel of the annunciation), but he is twice as good as that when he is relaxed and easy. He had strokes of brilliance last night, but the long easy stride of his earlier performance is on a plane with Miss Taylor's playing and gives the play greater strength.

Mr. Ross enters late, but leaves an impression as unforgettable as his green coat and his face, which is perilously close to being a mug. Late of "Winged Victory," this stalwart actor does a superb job as the gentleman caller who finds his visit a little more than he bargained for. Which leaves only Julie Haydon and there, frankly, I'm puzzled. At times she has the frailty of the glass animals of the title which are her refuge from reality. But I couldn't quite believe her, and my sympathy went to her nagging mother and her frustrated brother—because whatever the writing, acting is the final word, and they acted circles around her.

THE CATASTROPHE OF SUCCESS

This winter marked the third anniversary of the Chicago opening of *The Glass Menagerie,* an event which terminated one part of my life and began another about as different in all external circumstances as could well be imagined. I was snatched out of virtual oblivion and thrust into sudden prominence, and from the precarious tenancy of furnished rooms about the country I was removed to a suite in a first-class Manhattan hotel. My experience was not unique. Success has often come that abruptly into the lives of Americans. The Cinderella story is our favorite national myth, the cornerstone of the film industry if not of the Democracy itself. I have seen it enacted on the screen so often that I am now inclined to yawn at it, not with disbelief but with an attitude of Who Cares! Anyone with such beautiful teeth and hair as the screen protagonist of such a story was bound to have a good time one way or another, and you could bet your bottom dollar and all the tea in China that that one would not be caught dead or alive at any meeting involving a social conscience.

No, my experience was not exceptional, but neither was it quite ordinary, and if you are willing to accept the somewhat eclectic proposition that I had not been writing with such an experience in mind—and many people are not willing to believe that a playwright is interested in anything but popular success—there may be some point in comparing the two estates.

The sort of life which I had had previous to this popular success was one that required endurance, a life of clawing and scratching along a sheer surface and holding on tight with raw fingers to every inch of rock higher than the one caught hold of before, but it was a good life because it was the sort of life for which the human organism is created.

I was not aware of how much vital energy had gone into this struggle until the struggle was removed. I was out on a level plateau with my arm still thrashing and my lungs still grabbing at air that no longer resisted. This was security at last.

I sat down and looked about me and was suddenly very depressed. I thought to myself, this is just a period of adjustment. Tomorrow morning I will wake up in this first-class hotel suite above the discreet hum of an East Side boulevard and I will appreciate its elegance and luxuriate in its comforts and know that I have arrived at our American plan of Olympus. Tomorrow morning when I look at the green satin sofa I will fall in love with it. It is only temporarily that the green satin looks like slime on stagnant water.

But in the morning the inoffensive little sofa looked more revolting than the night before, and I was already getting too fat for the $125 suit which a fashionable acquaintance had selected for me. In the suite things began to break accidentally. An arm came off the sofa. Cigarette burns appeared on the polished surface of the furniture. Windows were left open and a rainstorm flooded the suite. But the maid always put it straight and the patience of the management was inexhaustible. Late parties could not offend them seriously. Nothing short of a demolition bomb seemed to bother my neighbors.

I lived on room service. But in this, too, there was a disenchantment. Some time between the moment when I ordered dinner over the phone and when it was rolled into my living room like a corpse on a rubber-wheeled table, I lost all interest in it. Once I ordered a sirloin steak and a chocolate sundae, but everything was so cunningly disguised on the table that I mistook the chocolate sauce for gravy and poured it over the sirloin steak.

Of course all this was the more trivial aspect of a spiritual dislocation that began to manifest itself in far more disturbing ways. I soon found myself becoming indifferent to people. A well of cynicism rose in me. Conversations all sounded as if they had been recorded years ago and were being played back on a turntable. Sincerity and kindliness seemed to have gone out of my friends' voices. I suspected them of hypocrisy. I stopped calling them, stopped seeing them. I was impatient of what I took to be inane flattery.

I got so sick of hearing people say, "I loved your play!" that I could not say thank you any more. I choked on the words and turned rudely away from the usually sincere person. I no longer felt any pride in the play itself but began to dislike it, probably because I felt too lifeless inside ever to create another. I was walking around dead in my shoes and I knew it but there were no friends I knew or trusted sufficiently, at that time, to take them aside and tell them what was the matter.

This curious condition persisted about three months, till late spring, when I decided to have another eye operation mainly because of the excuse it gave me to withdraw from the world behind a gauze mask. It was my fourth eye operation, and perhaps I should explain that I had been afflicted for about five years with a cataract on my left eye which required a series of needling operations and finally an operation on the muscle of the eye. (The eye is still in my head. So much for that.)

Well, the gauze mask served a purpose. While I was resting in the hospital the friends whom I had neglected or affronted in one way or another began to call on me, and now that I was in pain and darkness, their voices seemed to have changed, or rather that unpleasant mutation which I had suspected earlier in the season had now disappeared and they sounded now as they had used to sound in the lamented days of my obscurity. Once more they were sincere and kindly voices with the ring of truth in them and that quality of understanding for which I had originally sought them out.

As far as my physical vision was concerned, this last operation was only relatively successful (although it left me with an apparently clear black pupil in the right position, or nearly so) but in another, figurative way, it had served a much deeper purpose.

When the gauze mask was removed I found myself in a readjusted world. I checked out of the handsome suite at the first-class hotel, packed my papers and a few incidental belongings, and left for Mexico, an elemental country where you can quickly forget the false dignities and conceits imposed by success, a country where vagrants innocent as children curl up to sleep on the pavements and human voices, especially when their language is not familiar to the ear, are soft as birds'. My public self, that artifice of mirrors, did not exist here and so my natural being was resumed.

Then, as a final act of restoration, I settled for a while at Chapala to work on a play called *The Poker Night,* which later became *A Streetcar Named Desire.* It is only in his work that an artist can find reality and satisfaction, for the actual world is less intense than the world of his invention, and consequently his life, without recourse to violent disorder, does not seem very substantial. The right condition for him is that in which his work is not only convenient but unavoidable.

For me a convenient place to work is a remote place among strangers where there is good swimming. But life should require a certain minimal effort. You should not have too many people waiting on you; you should have to do most things for yourself. Hotel service is embarrassing. Maids, waiters, bellhops, porters, and so forth are the most embarrassing people in the world for they continually remind you of inequities which we accept as the proper thing. The sight of an ancient woman, gasping and wheezing as she drags a heavy pail of water down a hotel corridor to mop up the mess of some drunken overprivileged guest, is one that sickens and weighs upon the heart and withers it with shame for this world in which it is not only tolerated but regarded as proof positive that the wheels of Democracy are functioning as they should without interference from above or below. Nobody should have to clean up anybody else's mess in this world. It is terribly bad for both parties, but probably worse for the one receiving the service.

I have been corrupted as much as anyone else by the vast number of menial services which our society has grown to expect and depend on. We should do for ourselves or let the machines do for us—the glorious technology that is supposed to be the new light of the world. We are like a man who has bought a great amount of equipment for a camping trip, who has the canoe and the tent and the fishing lines and the axe and the guns, the mackinaw and the blankets, but who now, when all the preparations and the provisions are piled expertly together, is suddenly too timid to set out on the journey but remains where he was yesterday and the day before and day before that, looking suspiciously through white lace curtains at the clear sky he distrusts. Our great technology is a God-given chance for adventure and for progress which we are afraid to attempt. Our ideas and our ideals remain exactly what they were and where they were three centuries ago. No. I beg your pardon. It is no longer safe for a man to even declare them!

This is a long excursion from a small theme into a large one which I did not intend to make, so let me go back to what I was saying before.

This is an oversimplification. One does not escape that easily from the seduction of an effete way of life. You cannot arbitrarily say to yourself, I will now continue my life as it was before this thing, Success, happened to me. But once you fully apprehend the vacuity of a life without struggle you are equipped with the basic means of salvation. Once you know this is true, that the heart of man, his body and his brain, are forged in a white-hot furnace for the purpose of conflict (the struggle of creation) and that with the conflict removed, the man is a sword cutting daisies, that not privation but luxury is the wolf at the door and that the fangs of this wolf are all the little vanities and conceits and laxities that Success is heir to—why, then with this knowledge you are at least in a position of knowing where danger lies.

You know, then, that the public Somebody you are when you "have a name" is a fiction created with mirrors and that the only somebody worth being is the solitary and unseen you that existed from your first breath and which is the sum of your actions and so is constantly in a state of becoming under your own volition— and knowing these things, you can even survive the catastrophe of Success!

It is never altogether too late, unless you embrace the Bitch Goddess, as William James called her, with both arms and find in her smothering caresses exactly what the homesick little boy in you always wanted, absolute protection and utter effortlessness. Security is a kind of death, I think, and it can come to you in a storm of royalty checks beside a kidney-shaped pool in Beverly Hills or anywhere at all that is removed from the conditions that made you an artist, if that's what you are or were or intended to be. Ask anyone who has experienced the kind of success I am talking about—What good is it? Perhaps to get an honest answer you will have to give him a shot of truth serum but the word he will finally groan is unprintable in genteel publications.

Then what is good? The obsessive interest in human affairs, plus a certain amount of compassion and moral conviction, that first made the experience of living something that must be translated into pigment or music or bodily movement or poetry or prose or anything that's dynamic and expressive—that's what's good for you if you're at all serious in your aims. William Saroyan wrote a great play on this theme, that purity of heart is the one success worth having. "In the time of your life—live!" That time is short and it doesn't return again. It is slipping away while I write this and while you read it, and the monosyllable of the clock is Loss, loss, loss, unless you devote your heart to its opposition.

1947

ARCHIVAL
PRODUCTION
PHOTOGRAPHS
OF
*THE GLASS
MENAGERIE*

CHICAGO STAGEBILL

Laurette Taylor, Eddie Dowling, and Julie Hayden
featured on the program from the original Chicago production, 1944.
(*Photo courtesy of The Historic New Orleans Collection.*)

Julie Hayden as Laura and Anthony Ross as the Gentleman Caller
in the original Broadway production, 1945.
(*Photo courtesy of the Publicity Department at New Directions.*)

Arthur Kennedy as Tom and Gertrude Lawrence as Amanda
in a publicity still from the 1950 film adaptation.
(*Photo courtesy of the Publicity Department at New Directions.*)

Jane Wyman as Laura in a publicity still from the 1950 film adaptation.
(*Photo courtesy of the Publicity Department at New Directions.*)

Katharine Hepburn as Amanda and Sam Waterston as Tom
in the 1973 television production. (*Photo courtesy
of the Publicity Department at New Directions.*)

Maureen Stapleton as Amanda and George Grizzard as Tom
in the 1965 Broadway revival. (*Photo by Werner J. Kuhn,
courtesy of The Historic New Orleans Collection.*)

Piper Laurie as Laura and Jo Van Fleet, who replaced Maureen Stapleton
as Amanda, in the 1965 Broadway revival.
(*Photo courtesy of The Historic New Orleans Collection.*)

PORTRAIT OF A GIRL IN GLASS

We lived in a third floor apartment on Maple Street in Saint Louis, on a block which also contained the Ever-ready Garage, a Chinese laundry, and a bookie shop disguised as a cigar store.

Mine was anomalous character, one that appeared to be slated for radical change or disaster, for I was a poet who had a job in a warehouse. As for my sister Laura, she could be classified even less readily than I. She made no positive motion toward the world but stood at the edge of the water, so to speak, with feet that anticipated too much cold to move. She'd never have budged an inch, I'm pretty sure, if my mother who was a relatively aggressive sort of woman had not shoved her roughly forward, when Laura was twenty years old, by enrolling her as a student in a nearby business college. Out of her "magazine money" (she sold subscriptions to women's magazines), Mother had paid my sister's tuition for a term of six months. It did not work out. Laura tried to memorize the typewriter keyboard, she had a chart at home, she used to sit silently in front of it for hours, staring at it while she cleaned and polished her infinite number of little glass ornaments. She did this every evening after dinner. Mother would caution me to be very quiet. "Sister is looking at her typewriter chart!" I felt somehow that it would do her no good, and I was right. She would seem to know the positions of the keys until the weekly speed drill got underway, and then they would fly from her mind like a bunch of startled birds.

At last she couldn't bring herself to enter the school any more. She kept this failure a secret for a while. She left the house each morning as before and spent six hours walking around the park. This was in February, and all the walking outdoors regardless of weather brought on influenza. She was in bed for a couple of weeks with a curiously happy little smile on her face. Of course Mother phoned the business college to let them know she was ill. Whoever was talking on the other end of the line had some trouble, it seems, in remembering who Laura was, which annoyed my mother and she spoke up pretty sharply. "Laura has been attending that school of yours for two months, you certainly ought to recognize her name!" Then came the stunning disclosure. The person sharply retorted, after a moment or two, that now she *did* remember the Wingfield girl, and that she had not been at the business college *once* in about a month. Mother's voice became strident. Another person was brought to the phone to verify the statement of the first. Mother hung up and went to Laura's bedroom where she lay with a tense and frightened look in place of the faint little smile. Yes, admitted my sister, what they said was true. "I couldn't go any longer, it scared me too much, it made me sick at the stomach!"

After this fiasco, my sister stayed at home and kept in her bedroom mostly. This was a narrow room that had two windows on a dusky areaway between two wings of the building. We called this areaway Death Valley for a reason that seems worth telling. There were a great many alley cats in the neighborhood and one particularly vicious dirty white Chow who stalked them continually. In the open or on the fire escapes they could usually elude him but now and again he cleverly contrived to run some youngster among them into the cul-de-sac of this narrow areaway at the far end of which, directly beneath my sister's bedroom windows, they made the blinding discovery that what had appeared to be an avenue of escape was really a locked arena, a gloomy vault of concrete and brick with walls too high for any cat to spring, in which they must suddenly turn to spit at their death until it was hurled upon them. Hardly a week went by without a repetition of this violent drama, The areaway had grown to be hateful to Laura because she could not look out on it without recalling the screams and the snarls of killing. She kept the shades drawn down, and as Mother would not permit the use of electric current except when needed, her days were spent almost in perpetual twilight. There were three pieces of dingy ivory furniture in the room, a bed, a bureau, a chair. Over the bed was a remarkably bad religious painting, a very effeminate head of Christ with teardrops visible just below the eyes. The charm of the room was produced by my sister's collection of glass. She loved colored glass and had covered the walls with shelves of little glass articles, all of them light and delicate in color. These she washed and polished with endless care. When you entered the room there was always this soft, transparent radiance in it which came from the glass absorbing whatever faint light came through the shades on Death Valley. I have no idea how many articles there were of this delicate glass. There must have been hundreds of them. But Laura could tell you exactly. She loved each one.

She lived in a world of glass and also a world of music. The music came from a 1920 victrola and a bunch of records that dated from about the same period, pieces such as "Whispering" or "The Love Nest" or "Dardanella." These records were souvenirs of our father, a man whom we barely remembered, whose name was spoken rarely. Before his sudden and unexplained disappearance from our lives, he had made this gift to the household, the phonograph and the records, whose music remained as a sort of apology for him. Once in a while, on payday at the warehouse, I would bring home a new record. But Laura seldom cared for these new records, maybe because they reminded her too much of the noisy tragedies in Death Valley or the speed drills at the business college. The tunes she loved were the ones she had always heard. Often she sang to herself at night in her bedroom. Her voice was thin, it usually wandered off-key. Yet it had a curious childlike sweetness. At eight o'clock in the evening I sat down to write in my own mousetrap of a room. Through the closed doors, through the walls, I would hear my sister singing to herself, a piece like "Whispering" or "I Love You" or "Sleepy Time Gal," losing the tune now and then but always preserving the minor atmosphere of the music. I think that was why I always wrote such strange and sorrowful poems in those days. Because I had in my ears the wispy sound of my sister serenading her pieces of colored glass, washing them while she sang or merely looking down at them with her vague blue eyes until the points of gem-like radiance in them gently drew the arching particles of reality from her mind and finally produced a state of hypnotic calm in which she even stopped singing or washing the glass and merely sat without motion until my mother knocked at the door and warned her against the waste of electric current.

I don't believe that my sister was actually foolish. I think the petals of her mind had simply closed through fear, and it's no telling how much they had closed upon in the way of secret wisdom. She never talked very much, not even to me, but once in a while she did pop out with something that took you by surprise.

After work at the warehouse or after I'd finished my writing in the evening, I'd drop in her room for a little visit because she had a restful and soothing effect on nerves that were worn rather thin from trying to ride two horses simultaneously in two opposite directions.

I usually found her seated in the straight-back ivory chair with a piece of glass cupped tenderly in her palm.

"What are you doing? Talking to it?" I asked.

"No," she answered gravely, "I was just looking at it."

On the bureau were two pieces of fiction which she had received as Christmas or birthday presents. One was a novel called *The Rose-Garden Husband* by someone whose name escapes me. The other was *Freckles* by Gene Stratton Porter. I never saw her reading *The Rose-Garden Husband,* but the other book was one that she actually lived with. It had probably never occurred to Laura that a book was something you read straight through and then laid aside as finished. The character Freckles, a one-armed orphan youth who worked in a lumber camp, was someone that she invited into her bedroom now and then for a friendly visit just as she did me. When I came in and found this novel open upon her lap, she would gravely remark that Freckles was having some trouble with the foreman of the lumber camp or that he had just received an injury to his spine when a tree fell on him. She frowned with genuine sorrow when she reported these misadventures of her story-book hero, possibly not recalling how successfully he came through them all, that the injury to the spine fortuitously resulted in the discovery of rich parents and that the bad-tempered foreman had a heart of gold at the end of the book. Freckles became involved in romance with a girl he called The Angel, but my sister usually stopped reading when this girl became too prominent in the story. She closed the book or turned back to the lonelier periods in the orphan's story. I only remember her making one reference to this heroine of the novel. "The Angel is nice," she said, "but seems to be kind of conceited about her looks."

Then one time at Christmas, while she was trimming the artificial tree, she picked up the Star of Bethlehem that went on the topmost branch and held it gravely toward the chandelier.

"Do stars have five points really?" she enquired.

This was the sort of thing that you didn't believe and that made you stare at Laura with sorrow and confusion.

"No," I told her, seeing she really meant it, "they're round like the earth and most of them much bigger."

She was gently surprised by this new information. She went to the window to look up at the sky which was, as usual during Saint Louis winters, completely shrouded by smoke.

"It's hard to tell," she said, and returned to the tree.

So time passed on till my sister was twenty-three. Old enough to be married, but the fact of the matter was she had never even had a date with a boy. I don't believe this seemed as awful to her as it did to Mother.

At breakfast one morning Mother said to me, "Why don't you cultivate some nice young friends? How about down at the warehouse?

Aren't there some young men down there you could ask to dinner?"

This suggestion surprised me because there was seldom quite enough food on her table to satisfy three people. My mother was a terribly stringent housekeeper, God knows we were poor enough in actuality, but my mother had an almost obsessive dread of becoming even poorer. A not unreasonable fear since the man of the house was a poet who worked in a warehouse, but one which I thought played too important a part in all her calculations.

Almost immediately Mother explained herself.

"I think it might be nice," she said, "for your sister."

I brought Jim home to dinner a few nights later. Jim was a big red-haired Irishman who had the scrubbed and polished look of well-kept chinaware. His big square hands seemed to have a direct and very innocent hunger for touching his friends. He was always clapping them on your arms or shoulders and they burned through the cloth of your shirt like plates taken out of an oven. He was the best-liked man in the warehouse and oddly enough he was the only one that I was on good terms with. He found me agreeably ridiculous I think. He knew of my secret practice of retiring to a cabinet in the lavatory and working on rhyme schemes when work was slack in the warehouse, and of sneaking up on the roof now and then to smoke my cigarette with a view across the river at the undulant open country of Illinois. No doubt I was classified as screwy in Jim's mind as much as in the others', but while their attitude was suspicious and hostile when they first knew me, Jim's was warmly tolerant from the beginning. He called me Slim, and gradually his cordial acceptance drew the others around, and while he remained the only one who actually had anything to do with me, the others had now begun to smile when they saw me as people smile at an oddly fashioned dog who crosses their path at some distance.

Nevertheless it took some courage for me to invite Jim to dinner. I thought about it all week and delayed the action till Friday noon, the last possible moment, as the dinner was set for that evening.

"What are you doing tonight?" I finally asked him.

"Not a God damn thing," said Jim. "I had a date but her Aunt took sick and she's hauled her freight to Centralia!"

"Well," I said, "why don't you come over for dinner?"

"Sure!" said Jim. He grinned with astonishing brightness.

I went outside to phone the news to Mother.

Her voice that was never tired responded with an energy that made the wires crackle.

"I suppose he's Catholic?" she said.

"Yes," I told her, remembering the tiny silver cross on his freckled chest.

"Good!" she said. "I'll bake a salmon loaf!"

And so we rode home together in his jalopy.

I had a curious feeling of guilt and apprehension as I led the lamb-like Irishman up three flights of cracked marble steps to the door of Apartment F, which was not thick enough to hold inside it the odor of baking salmon.

Never having a key, I pressed the bell.

"Laura!" came Mother's voice. "That's Tom and Mr. Delaney! Let them in!"

There was a long, long pause.

"Laura?" she called again. "I'm busy in the kitchen, you answer the door!"

Then at last I heard my sister's footsteps. They went right past the door at which we were standing and into the parlor. I heard the creaking noise of the phonograph crank. Music commenced. One of the oldest records, a march of Sousa's, put on to give her the courage to let in a stranger.

The door came timidly open and there she stood in a dress from Mother's wardrobe, a black chiffon ankle-length and high-heeled slippers on which she balanced uncertainly like a tipsy crane of melancholy plumage. Her eyes stared back at us with a glass brightness and her delicate wing-like shoulders were hunched with nervousness.

"Hello!" said Jim, before I could introduce him.

He stretched out his hand. My sister touched it only for a second.

"Excuse me!" she whispered, and turned with a breathless rustle back to her bedroom door, the sanctuary beyond it briefly revealing itself with the tinkling, muted radiance of glass before the door closed rapidly but gently on her wraithlike figure.

Jim seemed to be incapable of surprise.

"Your sister?" he asked.

"Yes, that was her," I admitted. "She's terribly shy with strangers."

"She looks like you,' said Jim, "except she's pretty."

Laura did not reappear till called to dinner. Her place was next to Jim at the drop-leaf table and all through the meal her figure was slightly tilted away from his. Her face was feverishly bright and one eyelid, the one on the side toward Jim, had developed a nervous wink. Three times in the course of the dinner she dropped her fork on her plate with a terrible clatter and she was continually raising the water glass to her lips for hasty little gulps. She went on doing this even after the water was gone from the glass. And her handling of the silver became more awkward and hurried all the time.

I thought of nothing to say.

To Mother belonged the conversational honors, such as they were. She asked the caller about his home and family. She was delighted to learn that his father had a business of his own, a retail shoe store somewhere in Wyoming. The news that he went to night school to study accounting was still more edifying. What was his heart set on beside the warehouse? Radio-engineering? My, my, my! It was easy to see that here was a very up-and-coming young man who was certainly going to make his place in the world!

Then she started to talk about her children. Laura, she said, was not cut out for business. She was domestic, however, and making a home was really a girl's best bet.

Jim agreed with all this and seemed not to sense the ghost of an implication. I suffered through it dumbly, trying not to see Laura trembling more and more beneath the incredible unawareness of Mother.

And bad as it was, excruciating in fact, I thought with dread of the moment when dinner was going to be over, for then the diversion of food would be taken away, we would have to go into the little steam-heated parlor. I fancied the four of us having run out of talk, even Mother's seemingly endless store of questions about Jim's home and his job all used up finally—the four of us, then, just sitting there in the parlor, listening to the hiss of the radiator and nervously clearing our throats in the kind of self-consciousness that gets to be suffocating.

But when the blancmange was finished, a miracle happened.

Mother got up to clear the dishes away. Jim gave me a clap on the shoulders and said, "Hey, Slim, let's go have a look at those old records in there!"

He sauntered carelessly into the front room and flopped down on the floor beside the victrola. He began sorting through the collection of worn-out records and reading their titles aloud in a voice so hearty that it shot like beams of sunlight through the vapors of self-consciousness engulfing my sister and me.

He was sitting directly under the floor-lamp and all at once my sister jumped up and said to him, "Oh—you have freckles!"

Jim grinned. "Sure that's what my folks call me—Freckles!"

"Freckles?" Laura repeated. She looked toward me as if for the confirmation of some too wonderful hope. I looked away quickly, not knowing whether to feel relieved or alarmed at the turn that things were taking.

Jim had wound the victrola and put on *Dardanella*.

He grinned at Laura.

"How about you an' me cutting the rug a little?"

"What?" said Laura breathlessly, smiling and smiling.

"Dance!" he said, drawing her into his arms.

As far as I knew she had never danced in her life. But to my everlasting wonder she slipped quite naturally into those huge arms of Jim's, and they danced round and around the small steam-heated parlor, bumping against the sofa and chairs and laughing loudly and happily together. Something opened up in my sister's face. To say it was love is not too hasty a judgment, for after all he had freckles and that was what his folks called him. Yes, he had undoubtedly assumed the identity—for all practical purposes—of the one-armed orphan youth who lived in the Limberlost, that tall and misty region to which she retreated whenever the walls of Apartment F became too close to endure.

Mother came back in with some lemonade. She stopped short as she entered the portieres.

"Good heavens! Laura? Dancing?"

Her look was absurdly grateful as well as startled.

"But isn't she stepping all over you, Mr. Delaney?"

"What if she does?" said Jim, with bearish gallantry. "I'm not made of eggs!"

"Well, well, well!" said Mother, senselessly beaming.

"She's light as a feather!" said Jim. "With a little more practice she'd dance as good as Betty!"

There was a little pause of silence.

"Betty?" said Mother.

"The girl I go out with!" said Jim.

"Oh!" said Mother.

She set the pitcher of lemonade carefully down and with her back to the caller and her eyes on me, she asked him just how often he and the lucky young lady went out together.

"Steady!" said Jim.

Mother's look, remaining on my face, turned into a glare of fury.

"Tom didn't mention that you went out with a girl!"

"Nope," said Jim. "I didn't mean to let the cat out of the bag. The boys at the warehouse'll kid me to death when Slim gives the news away."

He laughed heartily but his laughter dropped heavily and awkwardly away as even his dull senses were gradually penetrated by the unpleasant sensation the news of Betty had made.

"Are you thinking of getting married?" said Mother.

"First of next month!" he told her.

It took her several moments to pull herself together. Then she said in a dismal tone, "How nice! If Tom had only told us we could have asked you *both*!"

Jim had picked up his coat.

"Must you be going?" said Mother.

"I hope it don't seem like I'm rushing off," said Jim, "but Betty's gonna get back on the eight o'clock train an' by the time I get my jalopy down to the Wabash depot—"

"Oh, then, we mustn't keep you."

Soon as he'd left, we all sat down, looking dazed.

Laura was the first to speak.

"Wasn't he nice?" she asked. "And all those freckles!"

"Yes," said Mother. Then she turned to me.

"You didn't mention that he was engaged to be married!"

"Well, how did I know that he was engaged to be married?"

"I thought you called him your best friend down at the warehouse?"

"Yes, but I didn't now he was going to be married!"

"How peculiar!" said Mother. "How very peculiar!"

"No," said Laura gently, getting up from the sofa. "There's nothing peculiar about it."

She picked up one of the records and blew on its surface a little as if it were dusty, then set it softly back down.

"People in love," she said, "take everything for granted."

What did she mean by that? I never knew.

She slipped quietly back to her room and closed the door.

•

Not very long after that I lost my job at the warehouse. I was fired for writing a poem on the lid of a shoe-box. I left Saint Louis and took to moving around. The cities swept about me like dead leaves, leaves that were brightly colored but torn away from the branches. My nature changed. I grew to be firm and sufficient.

In five years' time I had nearly forgotten home. I had to forget it, I couldn't carry it with me. But once in a while, usually in a strange town before I have found companions, the shell of deliberate hardness is broken through. A door comes softly and irresistibly open. I hear the tired old music my unknown father left in the place he abandoned as faithlessly as I. I see the faint and sorrowful radiance of the glass, hundreds of little transparent pieces of it in very delicate colors. I hold my breath, for if my sister's face appears among them—the night is hers!

JUNE 1943 (PUBLISHED 1948)

THE PRETTY TRAP

(A Comedy in One Act)

The Pretty Trap was first performed on March 23, 2011 at the Southern Rep Theatre, New Orleans, as part of the Tennessee Williams/New Orleans Literary Festival's centennial tribute to Williams. It was directed by Aimée Hayes; the set design was by Ashley Sehorn; the costume design was by Laura Sirkin-Brown; the sound design was by Mike Harkins; the props were designed by Sarah Zoghbi; and the lighting design was by Joan Long. The cast, in order of appearance, was as follows:

AMANDA WINGFIELD	Rebecca Taliancich
LAURA WINGFIELD	Lucy Faust
TOM WINGFIELD	Sean Glazebrook
JIM DELANEY	Chris Marroy

Character Descriptions:

Amanda Wingfield, a perennial southern belle, transferred to more rigorous climate and conditions.

Laura Wingfield, her daughter, a shy and sensitive girl of eighteen who "needs to be pushed a little."

Tom Wingfield, her son, the dreamy type, who also needs pushing a little.

Jim Delaney, a gentleman caller, who represents dreams plus action, the man coming toward us. Needs pulling.

Author's Note: This play is derived from a longer work in progress, *The Gentleman Caller*. It corresponds to the last act of that play, roughly, but has a lighter treatment and a different ending.

The feeling of the play is nostalgic. It belongs to memory, which is softly lighted and not too realistic, and often has the quality of faint music. The curtain rises on the interior of Apartment F, third floor south, on Maple Street in Saint Louis, in a block that also contains the Ever-ready Garage, a Chinese laundry, and a bookie's shop disguised as a cigar store. It is early summer. There are billowing white lace curtains at the windows and the furnishings of the little apartment contrive to have a certain grace and charm in spite of their cheapness. The scene is played in two areas, downstage for the living room and upstage for the dining room. Portieres are between the two areas, which give the effect of a second proscenium or a stage within a stage. That faint music, which is the music of memory, is heard as the curtain rises.

AMANDA [*offstage*]: Don't come into the kitchen in your white dress! Go in front and relax till they get here.

[*A door at the back of the upstage area is opened and Laura comes in. She is a very slight and delicate girl of nineteen. She has a fugitive prettiness that could easily escape attention, that comes and goes, but sometimes could stab your heart. Probably the dress that she actually wore on this evening was not so lovely as that which memory gives her. She seems to move in a radiance of her own. Amanda enters the dining room with a bowl of jonquils, which she places between the candelabra on the drop leaf table. She is a middle-aged woman of great energy whose early prettiness was more emphatic than Laura's. She has relinquished none of the girlish vivacity that must have been so charming in her youth but now is a little comical or pathetic.*]

AMANDA: I was carrying jonquils the very first afternoon that I met your father. However it wouldn't be fair to blame that on the flowers. The Cutrere boy had driven me over to Clarksdale to see

179

old Agnes Hoskins who'd just had another stroke and couldn't talk. It depressed me so to see her in that condition, but on the way back we passed this field of jonquils, literally thousands of them. I made Dave stop the car, and I got out and gathered my two arms full. Dave was annoyed because I wouldn't put them down in the back seat of the car. I used them for a shield when he tried to kiss me. I didn't care to be kissed by Dave Cutrere! [*She laughs archly.*] But when I got home and entered the downstairs hall, still carrying all those jonquils in my arms— Well, there was your father, discovered for the first time, installing a telephone at the foot of the stairs. How much better it would have been if—! [*She crosses downstage to Laura.*] Still—I wouldn't have had a daughter as pretty as you! If I hadn't married that telephone man, who fell in love with long-distance. That hem's a little uneven—hardly noticeable though, I'll leave it alone. I've got to mix the dressing for the salmon and change myself and it's already five of six. Laura, you're almost as pretty as I used to be. It's early for white, but white's so lovely on you. You're so slender, Laura. It's better to start out slender, for life does put flesh on you. I'm very lucky that I can still wear misses. Turn around. Yes—it dips a little but men don't notice such things. You've never looked so pretty and maybe you'll never look so pretty again. So be on your best behavior; for once come out of the shell— Vivacity counts for so much!

LAURA: I feel all gone inside.

AMANDA: Laura! Why?

LAURA: You've made such a fuss—Mother, you don't even *know* him!

AMANDA: He's Tom's best friend at the warehouse, and before I suggested Tom's bringing him home to dinner, I took a trip down there to have a look at him. I had Tom point him out.

LAURA: Oh, Lord.

AMANDA: On the pretext of buying some bedroom slippers. I liked his appearance very, very much, clean-cut type of boy who studies radio engineering at night school. Impresses me as worth investigation!

LAURA: You make it seem like we were setting a trap.

AMANDA: All pretty girls are a trap, a pretty trap, and men expect them to be. *I* was *amused* when boys came bumbling around, and I had no pangs of conscience when it seemed like one would have the trap sprung on him!

LAURA: I feel so ashamed of being pushed at strangers.

AMANDA: You wouldn't have to be pushed if you weren't such a shrinking violet of a girl, more old-fashioned than I am! I don't know how you do it, but you're eighteen and never been out with a boy! Never *out* with one even. If you were an awkward, homely, stupid girl, that would be natural, Laura. But you're like a young green tree that's beginning to flower, and is it so evil to have somebody look at you?

LAURA: You make it seem so important. That's why I'm nervous about it.

AMANDA: Well, it might be important, you can never tell. I'm not only the practical member of this family, but the romantic one, too...

LAURA: What has romance got to do with this boy coming over?

AMANDA: Nothing if you're a nit-wit! Nothing if you're just going to sit there with your teeth in your mouth, like you did the night that I took you over to the Young People's league at the church, speaking to nobody so nobody spoke to you! Your sort of prettiness can't be depended on, Laura. It might go out as quickly as it came and leave you stranded in this little apartment. I put you in business college, worked like a trooper so I could pay the tuition. What did you do? Claimed it made you nervous, and so you quit.

LAURA: I'm always being pushed into something, something I don't want.

AMANDA: What do you want, then? Tell me.

LAURA: To be left alone. I'd like to live by myself.

AMANDA: Two courses are open to girls in your circumstances. Either they have a business career or get married. And I've given up on you ever getting a job!

LAURA: Well, give up on getting me a husband, too.

AMANDA: All right, very well, then. I won't live forever to make provisions for you. You'll wind up one of those—barely tolerated spinsters who live with their brothers' families and eat the crust of humility all their lives! That's the future you cut out for yourself when you take no advantage of anything done for you.

[*Laura bursts into tears. She runs out of the room.*]

LAURA [*calling back*]: I'm going into my room and I won't come out. I won't come out for dinner. And you can have the gentleman caller yourself!

AMANDA: Don't come out, then! Stay in that little mousetrap of a room the rest of your days as far as I am concerned. I'll make no effort if everything's resisted! I'll call no more old women up to buy the *Home Beautiful*! I'll work in no more bargain basements either! I'll be just as neurotic as you, young lady, stay and keep my nose in books all the time and let the world pass by!

[*The doorbell rings.*]

AMANDA [*looking panicky*]: Oh, my heavens, and I'm still in my house-dress! [*Crosses back.*] Laura, Tom's lost his door-key again and is ringing the bell. You'll have to let them in.

LAURA: I won't do it, let them in yourself.

AMANDA: I can't go to the door. Just look at me, will you!

LAURA: I can't either.

AMANDA: You'll *have* to!

LAURA: Well, I *won't*. I absolutely won't.

[*Bell rings again.*]

AMANDA: Laura Wingfield, I do not intend to answer that door. And that is final. If you don't open the door and let your brother and Mr. Delaney in, the bell will go on ringing till Doomsday and I'll not budge an inch! You know me well enough to be quite certain I mean it! [*Pause. Another ring. Laura's door opens and she slips out.*]

LAURA: I've been—crying.

AMANDA: I don't care what you've been, you will go to the door!

LAURA: Well, then, get out of sight if you don't want to be seen, and I don't blame you! You really look like a witch!

AMANDA: Is that so!— Young lady. You—serpent's tooth! I have you children to thank for a faded appearance! Making myself a slave, doing menial labor, cooking in a high-school cafeteria, working in a dirty bargain basement, selling subscriptions to horrible magazines over the phone! And you throw at me such—such—

LAURA: If you want me to answer the door, you'll have to let go of my arm!

AMANDA: I don't want you to do anything *ever*!— *Believe* me! [*She bursts into tears and crosses out rear door.*]

LAURA: I'll let them in, but I won't come to the table! [*Crosses downstairs to front door as Tom starts knocking.*]

LAURA: All right, all right! You don't have to break the door down. [*She opens the front door, admitting Tom and Jim. She stares coldly at Tom, ignoring Jim altogether.*]

LAURA: Did you forget your key?

TOM: I lost it.

LAURA: You'd lose your head if it wasn't fastened on.

TOM: Laura, this is—Jim.

LAURA: How do you do?

JIM [*heartily*]: Hello, there. I didn't know Shakespeare had a sister.

LAURA [*barely touching the hand he extends*]: Excuse me. [*She turns quickly and goes out.*]

JIM: What was the matter?

TOM: She's very shy.

JIM: Oh! It's unusual to meet a shy girl. She looks a little like you except she's pretty.

TOM: Thanks.

JIM [*following him into living room*]: This is a nice little place.

TOM: Ha—ha!

JIM: Well, it's home-like.

TOM: Look at the paper?

JIM: Give me the comic section.

[*Amanda calls from the rear.*]

AMANDA: Tom?

TOM: Yes?

AMANDA: Is that you and Mr. Delaney?

TOM [*ironically*]: No, Mother, it's Napoleon and Joan of Arc! [*He is evidently as little pleased by his part in the business as Laura.*]

AMANDA: Ask the young man if he'd like to wash his hands?

TOM: Would you?

JIM: I took care of that at the warehouse.

TOM: He says his hands aren't dirty, Mother.

AMANDA [*musically*]: Well, dinner is nearly ready. I'll be right in.

TOM: Don't break your neck. [*Jim glances over the paper.*]

JIM: Your mother has a nice voice. Southern.

TOM: She's sort of a perennial southern belle. [*Picks up front page of paper.*] Hitler's bit off another hunk of Europe. [*Jim laughs heartily.*]

TOM: What's funny?

JIM: It's Sadie Hawkins day!

AMANDA [*off*]: Laura, dear, I hope you're nearly ready. I'm putting things on.

[*Amanda enters the dining room with a salad bowl. She has changed into a summery, girlish frock that is sprinkled with*

flowers. The hair net is removed, and her head is a mass of ring-
lets, which are distinctly too youthful for her present appearance.]

AMANDA [*musically*]: Somebody seems to be having a mighty
good laugh in here! This is Mr. Delaney, I presume? Oh, don't get
up! I've heard such a lot of wonderful things about you! Only you
haven't got the *comfo'table* chair. Tom, you're such a poor host, seat-
ing Mr. Delaney in that straight chair. You sit there on the *sofa*! I'm
not going to say "Mr.," I'm going to skip formalities and call you—

JIM [*a little stunned by her animation*]: —Jim.

AMANDA: *Jim*! I've known so many nice Jims—in days gone by.
In fact I've never known a Jim that wasn't a darling! So you must be
one too! Now tell me—Tell me all your hopes and dreams! Don't
be frightened of me, I know I'm a rattle-trap, I have all the vivacity
in this house! And I'm greedy for information, just—just—*greedy*
for it! So tell me everything! Everything all at once! You work in the
warehouse? Of course—I *know* you do! But what's your position
there? The same as Tom's? Oh, no, it's better than Tom's, Tom's
told me that already! A shipping—shipping—?

JIM: —Clerk. Yes—shipping clerk.

AMANDA: Oh! That must be—nice! You—handle—*shipping*.
Tom, go tell Miss Wingfield to put the rest of the dinner on the
table. You've met Laura, my pretty little daughter?

JIM: She let us in.

AMANDA: Oh, yes! You'll have to excuse her for making a late
appearance. We have no servant and Laura prepared the dinner.
Thank heavens my daughter is more domestic than I was! I was a
giddy young thing, as pretty as Laura. A little prettier even, if you
can believe it!

JIM: It's not hard to believe.

AMANDA: Well, I was, and I married a handsome man. A very remarkably good-looking man. His picture's there! So you can see for yourself. Tom Wingfield the First, that gallantly smiling gentleman over the Victrola! [*Jim rises to look.*]

JIM: He certainly was good looking.

AMANDA: No doubt about that! A girl can do no worse than put herself at the mercy of—a handsome appearance! Character's what to look for in a man. Sterling qualities, that's what counts in the world! What was I telling you? Oh, yes Tom Wingfield, the children's father. They hardly remember his face! He just disappeared, walked off one morning and didn't come back that night. A few months later I received a postcard from Hawthorne, California, saying on it—"Working on a squab ranch!" Tell me, what is a squab ranch, do you know?

JIM: I guess it's a—

AMANDA: Place where they raise pigeons! Something like that! The most improbable statement in the world! And went on to say "I'll send you some money as soon as I get paid!" But, Mr. Delaney—the man was never paid! Ha-ha-ha! Must have *never* been paid . . . ha-ha-ha! Well, five years later another post-card came, this one from Mexico. Ha-ha-ha! The capital city of Mexico, with a picture of—parrots or something! Well—"Dear Amanda. Hope you're well and happy. Much love. Tom!" Ha-ha-ha! That was the last we heard of Tom Wingfield the First. So you can see that Tom Wingfield the Second has a lot to live up to, and let me tell you— *I've* had to scratch for existence! Don't let anyone tell you a woman deserted with children to take care of has a bed of roses! A bed of—*briers* I've lived in! But why am I telling you all my earthly sorrows, when there's so much that's *pleasant* to talk about? Tom—is Laura getting the dinner on the table?

TOM: No, she isn't.

AMANDA: *What?*—Oh!—Please excuse me. I guess that Laura hasn't finished—dressing. I must *see*. [*She flounces prettily out, her musical laughter still ringing.*]

TOM [*gloomily*]: You see what I mean? A perennial southern belle.

JIM [*recovering slowly*]: She can—*talk!*

TOM: Oh, yes.

JIM [*wiping his forehead*]: Wonderful—a woman like that!

TOM: Would you like to live with her?

JIM: Like to? Why not!

TOM: Well— [*Amanda trips back in the upstage area with some dishes.*]

AMANDA: Are you talking about me? Am I the subject of discussion in there? Mr. Delaney, do you think I'm awful? Do you think I'm a—Laura, dear? Everything's ready!

LAURA [*off*]: I'm not coming out! [*Amanda laughs quickly to cover up.*]

AMANDA: My children compare me to—No, I won't say, I won't tell you! You'd think they were cruel, and they don't mean to be cruel. It's just that I'm of a—different generation, a different background. I still belong to the South, to Mississippi, where there was—gentle—living! *Gracious* living! *Kindness!* I ought to learn to be cold in the northern way, but I much prefer to stay the way that I am! My children will have to put up with a silly old mother they say looks like a witch! [*Enters portieres.*] Mr. Delaney—Jim!— Do I look like a witch?

JIM [*abashed*]: A—what?

AMANDA: A *witch!* That's what they *call* me! I guess you wonder what I've done to deserve such—castigation! Well, I'll tell you! I've pushed, I've driven, I've given myself no rest! I've sold subscriptions over the telephone. I've worked as an artist's model at the Washington Art School, standing in cruel positions for hours of time! I've taken in sewing, I've cooked at the high school cafeteria down on Newstead. I've modeled for matron's dresses at Famous & Barr. I've hired myself out as a practical nurse to horrible invalid women who've pinched and scratched me and made me ashamed to be human! I've done all *those* things, which was very bad of me, and so I am now like a *witch!*—And my children tell me I am and— [*She nearly bursts into tears. Turning quickly.*] Dinner is—served! [*Composing herself, she turns quickly and makes a little cringing courtesy.*] Gentlemen—dinner is served!

[*Tom closes his eyes for a moment. Jim gets up awkwardly, quite at a loss.*]

[*Meltingly.*] Jim—Jim, Jim! I'm going to take your arm into dinner, just as if the band was playing and this was a banquet hall! Let's imagine it is a banquet hall, all decorated with—palms! And beveled glass around the ivory walls! And chandeliers, all blazing to blind our eyes! I made my debut in Vicksburg at such an affair! And in New Orleans I was presented to society in the old Saint Charles hotel. I happened to have rich relatives in both cities who made things lovely, lovely! The Cartwrights were the Cotton Kings of the South! That's all gone now, all changed—all fallen to pieces, and here I am—on Maple Street in Saint Louis. Now I'll relinquish your arm! You sit over there, that side of our little table. *Laura?—Laura, dear!* Tom, sit at the head of the table. It isn't a pheasant, it's just a—salmon loaf!

JIM: It sure looks good, Mrs. Wingfield. It sure does smell good, too.

AMANDA: Laura?— Oh, Laura, we're waiting to say grace for you! Please hurry dear! [*To Jim.*] Laura's my chief cook and bottle washer!

JIM: And what's Shakespeare?

AMANDA: Shakespeare?— Oh! You mean *Tom*. [*She gurgles and leans over to catch Tom's arm and presses her head prettily against his shoulder.*]

AMANDA: Why, Tom is my right-hand *bower!* Only I'm sorry to hear you call him Shakespeare. I'm afraid that means he's been writing down at the warehouse. He's already lost five jobs from not devoting himself to his work. And if he's going to lose this one— Well, I give up! *Laura!* We *can't* say Grace until you come to the *table!* [*Her eyes flashing.*] We *won't say* Grace until you come to the table!

[*The rear door opens and Laura comes shyly and haughtily into the dining room. Her face is flushed with nervousness and anger and she walks very stiffly, looking at no one.*]

LAURA [*coldly*]: Where is my place, please?

AMANDA: Next to our gentleman caller—the place of honor.

LAURA: —Oh. Is there room for two places on this side of the table?

AMANDA: It's such a tiny table, but we'll make room, don't worry. We just have to be chummy, and if our feet get tangled under the table, nobody's going to think anybody is flirting!

TOM [*enduring no more*]: Mother, if you'll keep still—I'll say the Grace!

AMANDA [*clutching her throat*]: *Excuse* me! [*She winks at Jim, then prettily folds her hands and bows her head.*]

TOM [*in a rapid mumble*]: "For these and all thy mercies, God's Holy Name be praised—Through Christ our Lord, Amen."

AMANDA [*catching her breath*]: Oh, how you race *through* it! Let's be seated, all. *I'm* kind of *hungry*. How about *you* all?

JIM: I can sure eat something.

AMANDA: I never saw a man that couldn't eat. [*Serving the peas.*] Laura, what pretty crystal beads you're wearing! [*Laura says nothing.*] Where did you get them, Laura?

LAURA [*angrily*]: I got them at the five and ten cent store!

AMANDA: Why, Laura, I thought—Why, I thought *surely* some rich old man had given them to you! [*To Jim.*] Neither of my children have any humor. In spite of the fact that I was always laughing as a girl, so much so that the Presbyterians in Blue Mountain thought my soul was damned! And their father—well—excessive sobriety was never *his* characteristic! He had *charm*, I'll have to say that for him. One poor girl was certainly swept off her feet. Tom, give Mr. Delaney that nice crisp piece off the end, and put a little parsley on each plate. It isn't put there just for ornamentation. My grandfather used to say, "Grass is only for cows!"—when given lettuce. A brilliant old gentleman!— Ran for Senator of Alabama! But—*drank!* Laura, please sit up straight at the table, don't hunch over like that! Both of you children, sit up straight at the table. [*Reaches over to give them each a pat.*]

LAURA [*icily*]: Mother—please!

AMANDA: Just look at Mr. Delaney and copy his posture. See how straight he is sitting! I think it's a mark of character, sitting up straight at the table. Mr. Delaney—Jim—I bet you've had some military training.

JIM: I haven't yet, Mrs. Wingfield. But from what you see in the papers, it looks like I might get some pretty soon.

AMANDA [*throwing up her hands*]: Oh! Don't talk about it! If there's a war and this country's drawn into it, I'll just *die!*— *Just!*—*die!*

TOM: Don't make rash promises, Mother.

AMANDA: No, I mean it. If Tom had to go off to war—!

JIM: I don't think Shakespeare would ever get in the army.

AMANDA: No? Why not?

JIM: Well—he's the dreamy type that wouldn't be useful.

AMANDA: The dreamy type! Oh, Tom—your *reputation! And* I so wanted my son to be known as a real live wire, the go-getter type!— Not dreamy. I tell you, we could *use* a wide-awake man in this establishment. Are *you* wide-awake, Mr. Delaney?

JIM: Me? I'm an old workhorse.

AMANDA: You and I! The workhorses of the world! My children are dreamers. I know you *are* wide-awake. I'll tell you a secret. I went down and looked at you.

JIM: Me?— Where?

AMANDA: At the warehouse. [*Laura drops her fork.*] I'd heard Tom speak of a nice young man at the warehouse, so when I was down to buy some bedroom slippers, I made him point you out! My, how you were working! It did me good to see such—application! For that's such a valuable thing the way things are! You can't—underestimate it. And Tom—so slow, so dreamy—not quite seeming to know where anything was! While you were bustling around with such—assurance . . .

JIM: The way I look at it is—

AMANDA: How do you look at it?

JIM: There's three types in the world.

AMANDA: Oh! Three? What are they?

JIM: One—the workhorses of the world.

AMANDA: —Oh.

JIM: They do what they're told to do and at the end of each day they're given some oats to feed on. Enough to provide the energy for tomorrow.

AMANDA: Mr. Delaney, you surprise me a little.

JIM: Yeah?— Why?

AMANDA: A statement like that—I mean, so—analyzing! But go on! What's number two?

JIM: Type number two is the drivers! The managers of the work-horses, and owners of them. They portion out the oats and lock up the stable door when the work day is over—open it in the morning. [*Grins.*] I've got this all figured out. But then there is type number three.

AMANDA: Which type is that?

JIM: The Dreamy Type.

AMANDA: My children?

JIM: —Shakespeare—like him, for instance! He doesn't fit into either classification. He can't work and he wouldn't drive.

AMANDA: Can't work?

JIM: Speaking—figuratively.

AMANDA: —Oh . . .

JIM: There's quite a number like him, won't drive and can't be driven, a monkey wrench in the works.

AMANDA: Oh, how awful!

JIM: But don't you see, Mrs. Wingfield, if the works aren't good, then a monkey wrench in them *is!*

AMANDA: No, I don't see at all, I think it is awful, to fit into such a worthless classification!

TOM: So I'm a monkey wrench! [*He grins.*] I'm glad to know I've got a definition!

AMANDA [*clapping a hand to her forehead*]: Oh, my goodness, a monkey wrench for a son! Mr. Delaney, have some more potatoes.

JIM: No, thank you, Ma'am.

AMANDA: What does your father do, Jim?

JIM: He has a retail shoe store in Wyoming.

AMANDA: Shoes! A commodity always in demand! And some day you'll take over, I suppose?

JIM: My heart is set on radio engineering. I feel there's a great day coming for television. It will be a field where the dreamy types and the dissatisfied workhorses can flash to the world original pictures of things, and make great changes.

AMANDA: But won't these "drivers" you speak of flash the pictures?

JIM: Not if we muscle in first, the dreamers and I.

AMANDA: According to what you say, you're not the dreamy type nor exactly the ordinary workhorse either.

JIM: That's right, Mrs. Wingfield.

AMANDA: Just what are you then?

JIM [*grinning*]: A combination, the beginning of an experiment
—dreams plus action, which is the next generation!

AMANDA: —Oh! [*She smiles uncertainly.*] That sounds very
exciting.

JIM: It is, I think. "All the world is waiting for the sunrise!"

[*The chandelier flickers and dims out.*]

AMANDA: Where was Moses when the lights went out! Do you
know the answer to that one, Mr. Delaney?

JIM: No. What is the answer?

AMANDA: In the dark! [*Jim laughs appreciatively.*] [*Amanda
gets up.*] How lucky we have these candles on the table.

JIM: Here's a match. [*Lights one of the candelabras.*]

AMANDA: Everybody just sit still, I'll take a look at the fuse-box.
Can you tell a burnt-out fuse when you see one, Mr. Delaney?

JIM [*following her*]: Uh-huh.

AMANDA: Tom! Did you pay that light-bill?

TOM: Why, I—*think* so—I'm not sure.

AMANDA: Oh, there we have it! It's no use even looking at the
fuse-box! The dreamy type neglected to pay the light-bill!

JIM [*laughing*]: Shakespeare probably wrote a poem on it.

AMANDA: Mr. Delaney, it isn't a joking matter. There's such a
high price for negligence in this world!

JIM: Maybe the poem will win a ten-dollar prize!

AMANDA: We'll just have candlelight for the rest of the evening.

JIM: Well, what's wrong about that?

AMANDA: Nothing except I'm a little out of patience with type number three! Come on, Dreamy Type, you and I'll clear the dishes. Laura, you take Mr. Delaney into the living room. [She thrusts the candelabra into Laura's hand. Laura looks helplessly at Jim. He grins.]

JIM: Come on, Laura. Let's have a look at those records. I don't suppose you got any Benny Goodman, or boogie-woogie numbers?

LAURA: I—I'm afraid not. They're all old records that came with the Victrola.

[They pass into living room. Amanda draws the portieres behind them. She can be heard indistinctly upbraiding Tom in the kitchen.]

JIM: The machine's a pretty old-timer.

LAURA: —Yes. [Still holding the candelabra.] Father bought it the day before he left. With all these records.

JIM [sorting through them]: "Whispering." "Dardanella." Where did he go?

LAURA: He was type number three. —Nobody knows.

JIM: Oh. Just disappeared?

LAURA: —Yes. He left the music—by way of apology for him. When he—fell in love with long distance! [She smiles slightly.] And so we—haven't bought any new ones.

JIM: Don't you like swing-music?

LAURA: It makes me think of the speed-drills we used to have at Rubicam's Business College, we typed to—very fast music, which made me nervous . . . I had to quit after a while, it made me so— Where shall I put the candles?

JIM: On the floor! [*She does.*] This is nice. This is very nice, I like it. [*He smiles at her gently.*] I like this place. I like you people, Laura. [*He laughs.*] You're—you're—out of the world!

LAURA [*looking shyly away*]: Are we?

JIM: You're shy, aren't you? Don't be shy with me, I'm nothing to be shy of. What do you do?

LAURA: —Do?

JIM: Yes.

LAURA: I—don't know.

JIM: You went to business college, and didn't like it—and now?

LAURA: I—stay home—mostly.

JIM: Here?

LAURA: —Yes.

JIM: —What goes on?

LAURA: —Why—nothing.

JIM: But—something must.

LAURA: —Why—nothing. Really—nothing.

JIM: Huh! [*He looks at her across the candelabra.*] You're— you're very pretty.

LAURA [*startled*]: What?

JIM: The dreamy type in a girl is—very attractive. What do you do?

LAURA: I told you—really nothing. Not since the business college —didn't work out.

JIM: But something else will.

LAURA [*sadly*]: I—suppose.

JIM: Sure. —*Sure!* Why—not everybody is—delicate—like *you!* [*He is sitting on the floor. Slides himself closer, leaning over the candles.*]

JIM: What *do* you do? I mean—You have dates, don't you?

LAURA: —I—

JIM: Go out with fellows?

LAURA: —No, I—

JIM: Don't?

LAURA: I—don't—get along very well—with people—strangers. I—don't meet people—often. I— [*Her voice dies out in confusion. She looks down at her hands clasped tightly in her lap.*]

JIM [*laughs very gently*]: Don't understand why not.

LAURA: The city is big and— Everybody is busy!

JIM: What do *you* do?

LAURA: You keep asking me that and—I don't know. I sketch in the park, I—have my glass collection.

JIM: A collection? Of glass?

LAURA: —Yes. [*She speaks a little more naturally.*]

LAURA: Little objects made out of glass, you know.

JIM: I've never seen any.

LAURA: Of course you have. —In windows.

JIM: Little glass objects, huh? Like what!

LAURA: Animals—mostly. Little—miniatures of them.

JIM [*grinning*]: Animals mostly!

LAURA: —Yes. I've hundreds of them. All around my bedroom on little shelves, and all in very light and—delicate colors. On sunny days—I live inside a—rainbow!

JIM [*laughs softly*]: Let me see them.

LAURA: I could—bring one out. Wait! I'll bring some out!

[*She rises quickly and gracefully and slips through the portieres. Jim laughs softly to himself. He kneels to wind the Victrola and put on a record. It is very worn and plays very faintly—"Whispering." Laura comes back in with a piece of glass cupped in her palm. Something has happened to Laura. Something secret and lovely has opened up in her face like the long delayed opening of a flower. Jim sees it as she steps between the portieres and stands graceful and hesitant and incredibly delicate in the light of the candles. He rises slowly to his feet, and there is a pause in which they look at each other across the candelabra. Laura laughs a little—tenderly and shyly. She half extends her hand with the piece of glass. Jim's face is grave—attentive.*]

JIM [*softly*]: What is it—Laura?

LAURA: Only one to give you an idea of them.

JIM [*slowly extending his hand*]: What is it?

LAURA: This one's a unicorn. Do you know what that is?

JIM: —No. —What?

LAURA: Something that doesn't exist in the world anymore.

JIM: —Oh!

LAURA: It used to, though, when the world was in its childhood.

JIM: It looks like a horse.

LAURA: It is a horse. With a horn.

JIM: —Oh. —That doesn't exist anymore.

LAURA: No. —All of this kind have—disappeared from the world. Gone like father—with only music behind them!

JIM: Yeah. I see what you mean.

LAURA: He's all that's left of the beautiful unicorn horses.

LAURA: He's white. He's *not* white, he's—blue—Spilled over white! The way snow is when it's—late in the afternoon. Now hold him up—You see how he catches the light? Oh, he loves it, loves it! He has a permanent place on the top shelf in the window, where the sun stays longest because he—*loves* it!—so.

JIM: But they're all gone, the others of—his description?

LAURA: —Yes.

JIM: He must be—lonesome.

LAURA: He *is!* He's very brave, though, and he doesn't complain about it. He stays on the shelf with the ordinary horses that don't have horns, and he seems to be getting along with them very nicely. I don't hear arguments going on among them!

JIM [*laughs, rather astonished*]: —No?—Well, well—No arguments—going on . . . [*He stares gravely at Laura, not at the orna-*

ment of glass. She draws it slowly back and closes her fingers gently around it.]

LAURA: You have to be careful, careful!— If you breathe—it *breaks!*

JIM: A fellow like me—couldn't touch it?

LAURA: Oh, I think *you* could!

JIM: You don't know very much about me yet.

LAURA: You told a good deal at the table.

JIM: I didn't think you were listening!

LAURA: Oh, I was!

JIM: I can't imagine what made me talk so much!

LAURA: I'm glad you did. Here! Hold him if you like!

JIM: I'd better not.

LAURA: Oh, please! [*He takes it gingerly.*]

LAURA: There now! You're holding it very gently!

JIM: I am right now. But most of the time—you wouldn't trust me with it?

LAURA: Most of the time—You'd hold it the same as I do!

JIM: The record's stopped. I'd better change the record.

LAURA: Play "Dardanella." That's my favorite record.

JIM: Okay. Let's—Let's dance!

LAURA: I've never danced. I wish that I knew how.

JIM: Would you—like to try?

LAURA: Why, I—yes, I'd love to! [*They bend simultaneously to change the record. They bump their heads together and both draw back with a slight laugh.*]

LAURA: You—*you* do it.

JIM [*staring at her*]: Sure—I better do it. [*He bows over the little machine and puts on "Dardanella."*]

LAURA [*faintly*]: Your hair is—pretty!

JIM: Don't say "pretty." That's more for a—girl. *Your* hair is *pretty.*

LAURA: Oh, mine's so fine, there's nothing I can do with it but— let it go!

JIM: It's— [*Touches it gently.*] awfully pretty.

LAURA: "Well I still think *yours* is. Now shall we—start dancing?

JIM: Yes.

LAURA [*laughs uncertainly and shyly*]: How do I—?

JIM: Just leave all that to me. Don't tighten up, just be relaxed and let me move you around.

LAURA: —Can you?

JIM: Sure I can!

LAURA: Why, yes, you—can!

[*They start to move about the room in a dance that is a little constrained at first but rapidly takes on freedom and grace: Laura laughs breathlessly as he moves her faster about the little candle-lit room.*]

JIM: Just, just—let yourself go!

LAURA: I'm stepping on you!

JIM: Don't mind that!

LAURA: Don't *you?*

JIM: *I'm* not made of glass!

LAURA: It feels so funny.

JIM: Is that why you're laughing?

LAURA: No, I'm—out of breath! Please, let's—stop for a minute! I—feel so—*funny!* [*She laughs breathlessly and can't stop, like water gone down the wrong way. He gradually lets her go. She retreats a step from him, still struggling to catch her breath. His arms extend uncertainly.*]

JIM: You're a awf'ly pretty—little—Girl!

LAURA: —What?

JIM: —Little—little—girl! Made out of *glass!* When it's—sunny—living in a— [*Takes her hands and draws her towards him.*] —Rainbow! [*He kisses her full and hungrily on the lips.*]

[*After a couple of moments in which the embrace endures with a curious, hesitant intensity only possible between two people who have never really kissed before—Amanda opens the portieres. She has a pitcher of lemonade in one hand. But she draws discreetly back and closes the curtains again.*]

JIM: —Was that—?

LAURA [*faintly*]: Mother.

JIM: Gosh, I— [*He crosses to portieres.*]

JIM: Mrs. Wingfield?

AMANDA [*delicately*]: —Yes—Jim?

JIM: Laura and I would like to go out for a walk, if you don't mind.

AMANDA: I? Mind? [*She laughs delicately.*] On such a lovely spring evening? What could be nicer! You children do just as you please. I want so much to see young people—happy!

JIM [*still a little bewildered by what has occurred*]: Well, I—would you like to? [*Turning shyly to Laura.*]

LAURA: *Oh!—Why*—what could be nicer?

AMANDA [*appearing in the portieres, wisely and benevolently smiling and smiling*]: The park is only a couple of blocks from here. Don't go in far, but the moon will make it lovely!

JIM: Let's do that then, why that's a—swell idea! [*He starts to the door. Returns to snatch up his coat.*]

AMANDA: Oh, yes, your coat and— Don't you think that Laura needs a wrap?

JIM: I don't think so.

LAURA [*still looking at Jim with wonder*]: No, no! I won't need any!

AMANDA [*slyly, the eternal procuress emerging*]: That light thin dress? That summer dress she's wearing?

LAURA: I won't need any! Honest, mother, I won't!

JIM: She won't need any! Honest Mrs. Wingfield! Let's go, Laura.

AMANDA: All right, then. You children run along. I'll leave the door open for you, but—don't be later than—midnight! [*They are into the outside hall. Amanda crosses softly to the door and closes it noiselessly behind them. She catches her breath and crosses to the window. Raises the blind and separates the curtains. Tom comes in.*]

TOM: Where are they now?

AMANDA [*her voice low and musical*]: Gone for a walk.

TOM: Yeah?

AMANDA: The young man's—already *kissed* her!

TOM: —Huh?

AMANDA: Yes! [*Amanda breaks into delicate girlish laughter. It ends on a high, triumphant note.*]

TOM: I declare—you're a witch!

AMANDA: But I *was* a girl. [*Crossing slowly to the portieres.*] Girls are a pretty trap! That's what they've always been, and will always *be,* even when *dreams* plus *action*—take over the world! Now—now, dreamy type— Let's finish the dishes!

THE CURTAIN FALLS. THE END.

IN THE MENAGERIE

Why are you reading *The Glass Menagerie*? Why has this simple portrait of an American family been translated into more than twenty languages and performed all over the world? Everyone has a mother and a father, and every family has its problems—but there is more to it than that.

If you've been exposed to literary theories that say you should consider only the text and ignore the autobiographical background, do not apply these to Tennessee Williams, because much of his work was conditioned by his family situation. Family was his perpetual subject. If you ignore his life, you may miss a deeper understanding of his work. Tennessee Williams was born Thomas Lanier Williams on March 26, 1911, in Columbus, Mississippi, and his family called him Tom. His mother and father, Edwina Estelle Dakin and Cornelius Coffin Williams, met and married in 1907. Tom's sister Rose was born in 1909 and his brother Dakin in 1919. Much of Tom's childhood was spent in Clarksdale, Mississippi where his maternal grandfather, the Reverend Walter Dakin, was rector of St. George's Episcopal Church. However, Tom's father moved the family to St. Louis in 1918, leaving behind a relatively idyllic small town for life in a modern American city.

I grew up in St. Louis before air conditioning as Williams did and can testify that in the 1930s it was one of the hottest places in the country in summer. Like both Tom Williams and the character of Tom Wingfield, many of us sought relief at the motion picture theaters such as the Tivoli and the Pageant that, unlike homes, were air-conditioned and offered the stage-show extras described in the play. Others took blankets to Forest Park to seek a few hours rest near its lakes.

Forest Park is important in Williams's plays. It was a constant in his youth since in most of their nine moves in St. Louis his family still remained near Forest Park. Larger than Central Park in New York, it had lakes, streams, botanical gardens, an excellent art museum, an outdoor municipal theater, and one of the first zoos in the country with natural settings. At the park's theater, "the Muny," Williams saw his first staged drama, and the fact that its productions combined acting with music and dance, offered comedy, tragedy and farce, and had large casts doubtless influenced Williams's early plays. (*Candles to the Sun,* his first full length play, has twenty speaking characters plus a mob scene.) The zoo, which Laura Wingfield in *Menagerie* visits daily in her truancy from business college, might be seen as a symbol of Tom Williams's family, each member trapped in a separate cage. In 1918 their move from Clarksdale Mississippi, a cotton center of about 6,000 people, to St. Louis, the sixth largest city in the United States where Cornelius would have a managerial job with International Shoe Company, the largest in the world, seemed an obvious advantage to him, who had been a traveling salesman. It would allow him time with his wife and to get acquainted with his son and daughter, who scarcely knew him.

To Tom, age seven, and Rose, little more than a year older, reared by loving grandparents in the peace of the Episcopalian rectory, the move was devastating. A tragic view of the move was encouraged by their mother who, despite being born in Ohio, had made herself into a Southern belle. She wore beautiful clothes, sewed by her mother, sang prominently in church, and was rather proud that her one culinary achievement was an angel food cake. The children, used to the small classes of Clarksdale schools and classmates of Anglo-Saxon background like their own, would go to large public schools in St. Louis with students of many nationalities where they would be mocked for their southern accents. Only sixteen months apart, Rose and Tom were so inseparable that they were called "the couple." Vivacious and attractive, Rose was the ringleader in any escapades, Tom the devoted follower. This relationship would change as Rose reached puberty and became increasingly unpredictable and strangely withdrawn. The climax of this behavior came during a recital duet where she played the piano, making increasing mistakes, and the young man accompanist to whom she was obviously attracted tried to cover for her on the violin, ending with her public breakdown. The disastrous duet is recorded in Williams's story, "The Resemblance Between a Violin Case And a Coffin" (1949). By her mid-teens Rose showed signs of clinical depression. She expressed fear of her father that developed into a phobia. In 1937 at age twenty-seven she was diagnosed as schizophrenic and put in the state insane asylum at Farmington. That same year Tom, at Washington University, published five poems to Rose in the College yearbook. In his playwriting class contest he entered a one-act play, *Me, Vashya* in which the heroine is mad.

The family tried to keep Tom away from his sister, fearing that her fate might become his as well. But Tom found his own salvation in writing. He got involved with the local radical theater group, The Mummers, for whom he wrote three plays, *Candles to the Sun, Fugitive Kind,* and *Not About Nightingales.* Successful productions of two of them encouraged him to go to the University of Iowa, which at that time had the best theater program in the country outside of Yale. Here he read the assigned one hundred plays each semester and turned in a required sketch every other week. After graduation at twenty-seven with no jobs to be found, he entered a playwriting contest for writers under twenty-five, conveniently subtracting three years off his age, and using for the first time the name Tennessee (instead of Thomas Lanier) Williams. Winning a prize in the contest brought him to the attention of Audrey Wood, the New York agent who started his career. Later, when Wood asked for a list of what he had written before 1943, he typed out a summary of titles for ten long plays (including a rough draft of *The Gentleman Caller*), sixteen short plays, twenty-five stories, "a large collection of verse," and "some others I can't recall." He was thirty-two. Wood got him a job in Hollywood at MGM paying the fantastic sum of $250 a week to write a "vehicle" for Lana Turner. But when he learned in January 1943 that, at the direction of his mother, his sister had undergone a pre-frontal lobotomy, he spent his time writing a film treatment called "The Gentleman Caller." He told MGM it would last longer than "Gone With The Wind." MGM fired him, but his prophecy about the script that became *The Glass Menagerie* came true.

Opening in Chicago on December 26, 1944, with Laurette Taylor as Amanda, the play moved to Broadway where it won the New York Drama Critic's Circle Award and the Sidney Howard Award of $1,500 and made Williams famous overnight. He was soon earning $1,000 a week in royalties. He signed over half the rights of *Menagerie* to his mother, enabling her to divorce Cornelius and buy a fine house in St. Louis County. For years she refused to see herself in the portrait of Amanda, even though the bossy and sometimes comic character in the play was redeemed by her capacious love for her children and her relentless survival instincts. Williams removed Rose from the asylum to a lodge in New York State where she had a private cottage and a live-in companion. He bought her beautiful clothes. All his life he would take her with him to important occasions, even to the Shubert Theatre in 1981 when he received the Commonwealth Award for his contribution to theater. Various aspects of Rose inform at least six of his plays, the most important being *The Glass Menagerie*. One of his late works, *The Two Character Play*, portrays a brother and sister who try to break the lifelong tie between them but cannot. As he grew older, Williams saw his father with more understanding and demonstrated his increasing empathy in a poignant essay, "The Man in the Overstuffed Chair."

With the years, his view of St. Louis also softened and he acknowledged its influence on his work. At least seven of his long plays are set in St. Louis, along with fourteen of his short ones and several more have St. Louis components. Before he died he could admit his debt to St. Louis: "I'm glad I spent those years there," he wrote, comparing them to the irritant in the oyster shell that forms the pearl and admitting that they had made him a writer.

Williams's call for "a plastic theatre" in his production notes for *The Glass Menagerie* is one of the manifestoes of modern drama and the play becomes even more important as its experimental qualities are understood:

> "The straight realistic play with its genuine Frigidaire and authentic ice-cubes, its characters who speak exactly as its audience speaks . . . has the same virtue of a photographic likeness. Everyone should know nowadays the unimportance of the photographic in art: that truth, life, or reality is an organic thing which the poetic imagination can represent or suggest, in essence, only through transformation."

Williams describes this plastic theatre that would use stage design, lighting, mime, dance and music in a symbolic way to reinforce the meaning of the play. He suggests the use of slides that would project comments on the action and wrote these into *Menagerie* but they were cut from the original production by director Eddie Dowling and are generally overlooked. He calls for "a single recurring tune, 'The Glass Menagerie,' between each episode of the play as 'Laura's music.'" For the original production the music was written by composer Paul Bowles but seldom is used, perhaps because it was not printed with the play.

As one might expect, *Menagerie*, as Williams's first important long play, showed influences from other sources such as Chekhov, whose simplicity he admired. Menagerie is a family portrait like Chekhov's The Three Sisters. He seems to have borrowed his play's title from Hart Crane's poem "The Wine Menagerie." The surprise is the influence of Rainer Maria Rilke, the a German lyric poet influenced by Baudelaire and the Romantics. Williams probably learned of him through his friend, Clark Mills, a published poet and linguist who greatly influenced Tom, introducing him to translations of the work of foreign writers. Williams evidently read J. B. Leishman's 1936 translation of Rilke's Sonnets to Orpheus that summer when Clark and Tom had their "literary factory" in Clark's basement and Clark introduced him to surrealism and French playwrights. Two of Rilke's sonnets actually describe the climax of Williams's play both in their portrait of Laura and the plot. Sonnet 25 reads:

> Now let me recall you, you whom I never
> knew except as a nameless flower, and try
> to show you just once to them all, abducted for ever,
> beautiful playmate of the invincible cry.
>
> Dancer at first, that suddenly, one hesitation,
> paused, with her youthfulness bronzed into art;
> mournfully listening.—Then the superior nation
> poured their music into her altered heart.
>
> Sickness was near. Already the shadows were greeting
> the darklier thrusting blood, but with only a fleeting
> doubt it surged to its spring-time, laughing at fate.
>
> Again and again out of darkness, emergent and mocking,
> it gleamed of the earth. Till after a terrible knocking
> it entered the hopelessly open gate.

Then, in Part Two, Sonnet Four:

> This is the creature that has never been.
> They never knew it, and yet none the less
> entirely loved it, from its suppleness
> to the very light of the eyes, mild and serene.
>
> It never was. And yet their love supplied
> the need of being. They always left a space.
> And in that clear space they had set aside
> it lightly raised its head and felt no trace

of not being real. They did not give it corn,
but fed it with their feeling that it *might*,
somewhere, exist. Were able to confer

such strength, its forehead grew a horn. One horn.
It came up to a virgin once, all white—
and lived on in the mirror and in her.

It's all here, the flower, Rose, Tom's sister and "beautiful play-mate" ("Laura" in the play), her approaching illness, her link as virgin to the unicorn, a veritable summary of the climax of Williams's play: the scene where The Gentleman Caller teaches Laura to dance. It seems likely that Williams got his inspiration from Rilke that summer of 1936. There is a great deal of symbolism in *The Glass Menagerie*: the glass animals, especially the unicorn, the fire escape, the absent father's portrait, the Victrola, the nickname "Blue Roses." The reader can speculate on the meaning of Laura's gesture when she gives the broken unicorn to her Gentleman Caller. Tennessee would read Rilke all his life. "I love Rilke," he told Cecil Brown who, interviewing Williams in 1974, noticed a copy of Rilke's *Duino Elegies* beside the typewriter in Williams's study.

The Centennial of Williams's birth, March 2011, will be celebrated in New Orleans, New York, Mississippi, Provincetown, in Nancy, France, and perhaps all over the world. To date, no plans have been made for a celebration in St. Louis, the city Tom Williams loved to hate but which he finally vindicated as the source of his inspiration. With its fire escape, the dark apartment on Westminster Place that housed his sister's little glass animals has been restored and renamed "The Tennessee Williams." A bronze bust of Williams sits nearby. A block away the Wednesday Club Auditorium where his first plays, performed by the Mummers, still stands. Designed by architect Theodore C. Link, it is in need of restoration. Nearby on Delmar, the Tivoli and Pageant theaters where Tom Wingfield went to the movies still operate. Near them is even a boarded-up dance hall, perhaps the one whose music Laura danced to with the Gentleman Caller. Forest Park, the sanctuary for both Tom and Rose Williams, is still an attractive refuge and its Municipal Opera still performs musicals. In Calvary Cemetery near the Mississippi River, Tennessee's grave is next to Rose's. Due to a mistake in spacing, they were almost buried together. On Tennessee's beautiful tombstone, overlooked by his mother's, he is identified as "Poet" and "Playwright" and it is inscribed with a line from his play *Camino Real* spoken by the character of Don Quixote: "The violets in the mountains have broken the rocks." And on Delmar in University City a sidewalk plaque in bronze says:

Tennessee Williams
One of America's Greatest Playwrights

I believe we can now leave out any qualification and say simply, "America's Greatest Playwright."

ALLEAN HALE
JULY 2011

THE HOMOSEXUAL IN SOCIETY

INTRODUCTION

Seymour Krim has urged me to reprint this early essay as "a pioneering piece," assuring me "that it stands and will stand on its own feet." At the time it was printed (*Politics*, August 1944) it had at least the pioneering gesture, as far as I know, of being the first discussion of homosexuality which included the frank avowal that the author was himself involved; but my view was that minority associations and identifications were an evil wherever they supersede allegiance to and share in the creation of a human community good—the recognition of fellow-manhood.

Blind lifeliness—what Darwin illuminates as evolution—has its creative design, and in that process a man's sexuality is a natural factor in a biological economy larger and deeper than his own human will. What we create as human beings is a picture of the meaning and relation of life; we create perspectives of space and time or a universe; and we create ideas of "man" and of "person," of gods and attendant powers—a drama wherein what and who we are are manifest. And this creation governs our knowledge of good and evil.

For some, there are only the tribe and its covenant that are good, and all of mankind outside and their ways are evil; for many in America today good is progressive, their professional status determines their idea of "man" and to be genuinely respectable their highest concept of a good "person"—all other men are primitive, immature, or uneducated. Neither of these perspectives was acceptable to me. I had been encouraged by my parents, by certain teachers in high school, by friends, through Socialist and Anarchist

Originally appeared in *Politics*, I, 7 (August 1944). The revisions were made in 1959. The expanded version was first published in *Jimmy & Lucy's House of "K,"* 3 (January 1985).

associations, and through the evidence of all those artists, philosophers and mystics who have sought to give the truth of their feeling and thought to mankind, to believe that there was an entity in the imagination "mankind," and that there was a community of thoughtful men and women concerned with the good of that totality to whom I was responsible. The magazine *Politics* represented for me during the Second World War an arena where intellectuals of that community were concerned, and I came to question myself in the light of the good they served.

It was not an easy essay to write. As a form an essay is a field in which we try ideas. In this piece I try to bring forward ideas of "homosexual," "society," "human" and, disguised but evident, my own guilt; and their lack of definition is involved with my own troubled information. Our sense of terms is built up from a constant renewed definition through shared information, and one of the urgencies of my essay was just that there was so little help here where other writers had concealed their own experience and avoided discussion.

Then too, the writing of the essay was a personal agony. Where we bear public testimony we face not only the community of thoughtful men and women who are concerned with the good, but facing the open forum we face mean and stupid men too. The involved disturbed syntax that collects conditional clauses and often fails to arrive at a full statement suggests that I felt in writing the essay that I must gather forces and weight to override some adversary; I have to push certain words from adverse meanings which as a social creature I share with the public to new meanings which might allow for an enlarged good. In the polemics of the essay it is not always possible to find the ground of accusation unless we recognize that I was trying to rid myself of one persona in order to give birth to another, and at the same time to communicate the process and relate it to what I called "society," a public responsibility. I was likely to find as little intellectual approval for the declaration of an idealistic morality as I was to find for the avowal of my homosexuality. The work often has value as evidence in itself of the conflict concerned and of the difficulty of statement then just where it is questionable as argument. I had a likeness to the public and shared its conflicts of attitude—an apprehension which shapes the course of the essay.

I feel today as I felt then that there is a service to the good in bringing even painful and garbled truth of the nature of our thought and feeling to the light of print, for what I only feel as an urgency and many men may condemn me for as an aberration, some man reading may render as an understanding and bring into the wholeness of human experience. Reading this essay some fifteen years later, I need courage to expose the unhappiness of my writing at that time, for I am not today without conflicting feelings and have the tendency still to play the adversary where I had meant only to explore ideas. In preparing the text then I have eliminated certain references that were topical at the time but would be obscure now and have cut where economy was possible without losing the character of the original; but I have not sought to rewrite or to remedy the effect.

[Robert Duncan's footnotes for the 1944 publication of this essay have been indicated by asterisks and set in a typeface different from the rest of the text. Duncan also added footnotes when he made revisions to the text in 1959. These notes have been indicated by numbers.]

THE TEXT

I propose to discuss a group whose only salvation is in the struggle of all humanity for freedom and individual integrity; who have suffered in modern society persecution, excommunication; and whose intellectuals, whose most articulate members, have been willing to desert that primary struggle, to beg, to gain at the price if need be of any sort of prostitution, privilege for themselves, however ephemeral; who have been willing rather than to struggle toward self-recognition, to sell their product, to convert their deepest feel-

ings into marketable oddities and sentimentalities.
Although in private conversation, at every table, at every edito-
rial board, one *knows* that a great body of modern art is cheated
out by what amounts to a homosexual cult; although hostile critics
have at times opened fire in attacks as rabid as the attack of Southern senators upon "niggers"; critics who might possibly view the
homosexual with a more humane eye seem agreed that it is better
that nothing be said.[1] Pressed to the point, they may either, as in
the case of such an undeniable homosexual as Hart Crane, contend
that he was great despite his "perversion"*—much as my mother
used to say how much better a poet Poe would have been had he
not taken dope; or where it is possible they have attempted to
deny the role of the homosexual in modern art, defending the good
repute of modern art against any evil repute of homosexuality.

But one cannot, in face of the approach taken to their own problem by homosexuals, place any weight of criticism upon the liberal
body of critics for avoiding the issue. For there are Negroes who have

---

*Critics of Crane, for instance, consider that his homosexuality is the cause of his in-
ability to adjust to society. Another school feels that inability to adjust to society causes
homosexuality. What seems fairly obvious is that Crane's effort to communicate his
inner feelings, his duty as a poet, brought him into conflict with social opinion. He
might well have adjusted his homosexual desires within society as many have done by
"living a lie" and avoiding any unambiguous reference in his work.

[1] 1959. At a round table on Modern Art held in San Francisco in 1949 a discussion
emerged between Frank Lloyd Wright and Marcel Duchamp where both showed
the courage of forthright statement, bringing the issue publicly forward, which I
lamented the lack of in 1944. *Wright* (who had been challenged on his reference
to modern art as "degenerate"): "Would you say homosexuality was degenerate?"
Duchamp: "No, it is not degenerate." *Wright*: "You would say that this movement
which we call modern art and painting has been greatly or is greatly in debt to ho-
mosexualism?" *Duchamp*: "I admit it, but not in your terms . . . I believe that the
homosexual public has shown more interest or curiosity for modern art than the
heterosexual—so it happened, but it does not involve modern art itself."
What makes comment complicated here is that, while I would like to answer as
Duchamp does because I believe with him that art itself is an expression of vitality,
in part I recognize the justice of Wright's distaste, for there is a homosexual clique
which patronizes certain kinds of modern art and even creates because, like Wright,

joined openly in the struggle for human freedom, made articulate that their struggle against racial prejudice is part of the struggle for all; there are Jews who have sought no special privilege or recognition for themselves as Jews but have fought for *human* rights, but there is in the modern American scene no homosexual who has been willing to take in his own persecution a battlefront toward human freedom. Almost coincident with the first declarations for homosexual rights was the growth of a cult of homosexual superiority to heterosexual values; the cultivation of a secret language, the *camp*, a tone and a vocabulary that are loaded with contempt for the uninitiated.

Outside the ghetto the word "goy" disappears, wavers, and dwindles in the Jew's vocabulary as he becomes a member of the larger community. But in what one would believe the most radical, the most enlightened "queer" circles, the word "jam" remains, designating all who are not wise to homosexual ways, filled with an unwavering hostility and fear, gathering an incredible force of exclusion and blindness. It is hard (for all the sympathy which I can bring to bear) to say that this cult plays any other than an evil role in society.[2]

they believe both homosexuality and the art they patronize and create to be decadent and even fashionably degenerate.

[2] 1959. The alienation has not decreased but increased when the "Beat" cult projects its picture of themselves as saintly—junkies evoking an apocalyptic crisis in which behind the mask of liberal tolerance is revealed the face of the hated "square." Their intuition is true, that tolerance is no substitute for concern; but their belief that intolerance is more true, dramatizes their own share in the disorder. "Goy," "jam," and "square" are all terms of a minority adherence where the imagination has denied fellow-feeling with the rest of mankind. Where the community of human experience is not kept alive, the burden of meaning falls back upon individual abilities. But the imagination depends upon an increment of associations.

Where being "queer" or a "junkie" means being a pariah (as it does in beat mythology), behavior may arise not from desire but from fear or even hatred of desire; dope-addiction may not be a search for an artificial paradise, an illusion of magical life, but an attack upon life, a poisoning of response; and sexual acts between men may not mean responses of love but violations of inner nature. Ginsberg (who believes the self is subject to society), Lamantia (who believes the self has authority from God), and McClure (who believes the self is an independent entity) have in common their paroxysms of self-loathing in which the measure of human failure and sickness is thought so true that the measure of human achievement and life is thought false.

But names cannot be named.[3] There are critics whose cynical, back-biting joke upon their audience is no other than this secret special reference; there are poets whose nostalgic picture of special

But this attitude had already appeared in the work of urban sophisticates like Edmund Wilson and Mary McCarthy where there was an observable meanness of feeling. Robert Lowell's "Tamed by Miltown, we lie on Mother's bed" expresses in the *realism* of neurotic inhibition what Allen Ginsberg's "Creation glistening backwards to the same grave, size of universe" expresses in the *surrealism* of psychotic exuberance. "Mother your master-bedroom/looked away from the ocean" and "O Mother . . . with your nose of bad lay with your nose of the smell of the pickles of Newark" dramatizes with the difference of class the common belief in oedipal grievance.

[3] 1959. That even serious socio-sexual studies are curbed is shown by the following letter written by an eminent poet when I wrote in 1945 asking if I could attempt an essay on his work in the light of my concept that his language had been diverted to conceal the nature of his sexual life and that because he could never write directly he had failed to come to grips with immediacies of feeling:

"... I am very sorry but I must ask you not to publish the essay you propose. I'm sure you will realize that the better the essay you write, the more it will be reviewed and talked about, and the more likelihood there would be of it being brought publicly to my attention in a way where to ignore it would be taken as an admission of guilt.

"As you may know, I earn a good part of my livelihood by teaching, and in that profession one is particularly vulnerable. Further, both as a writer and as a human being, the occasion may always arise, particularly in these times, when it becomes one's duty to take a stand on the unpopular side of some issue. Should that ever occur, your essay would be a very convenient red-herring for one's opponents. (Think of what happened to Bertrand Russell in New York.)

"I hope you will believe me when I say that for myself personally I wish I could let you publish it, and that anyway I hope the other essays will be as good as you would like them to be."

My own conviction is that no public issue is more pressing than the one that would make a man guilty and endanger his livelihood for the open knowledge of his sexual nature; for the good of humanity lies in a common quest through shared experience toward the possibility of sexual love. Where we attend as best we can the volitions and fulfillments of the beloved in sexual acts we depend upon all those who in arts have portrayed openly the nature of love; and as we return ourselves through our writing to that commune of spirit we come close to the sharing in desire that underlies the dream of universal brotherhood. Undeclared desires and private sexuality feed the possibility of sexual lust which has many betrayals, empty cravings, violations, and wants to void the original desire.

That this eminent poet was not wrong in speaking of his professional vulnerability were his sexual nature openly avowed can be verified by the following passage from a letter of an eminent editor after reading "The Homosexual In Society" concerning my poem "Toward An African Elegy" which he had previously admired and accepted for publication:

worth in suffering, sensitivity, and magical quality is no other than this intermediate "sixth sense"; there are new cult leaders whose special divinity, whose supernatural and visionary claim is no other than this mystery of sex.[4] The law has declared homosexuality secret, inhuman, unnatural (and why not then supernatural?). The law itself sees in it a crime—not in the sense that murder, thievery, seduction of children, or rape are seen as *human* crimes—but as crime against the way of nature.[*] It has been lit up and given an awful and lurid attraction such as witchcraft was given in the 17th century. Like early witches, the homosexuals, far from seeking to undermine

[*]"Just as certain judges assume and are more inclined to pardon murder in inverts and treason in Jews for reasons derived from original sin and racial predestination." *Sodom and Gomorrah*, Proust.

". . . I feel very sure we do not wish to print the poem, and I regret very much to decline it after an original acceptance. I must say for the record that the only right I feel in this action is that belatedly, and with your permission, I read the poem as an advertisement or a notice of overt homosexuality, and we are not in the market for literature of this type.

"I cannot agree with you that we should publish it nevertheless in the name of freedom of speech; because I cannot agree with your position that homosexuality is not abnormal. It is biologically abnormal in the most obvious sense. I am not sure whether or not state and federal law regard it so, but I think they do; I should not take the initiative in the matter, but if there are laws to this effect I concur in them entirely. There are certainly laws prohibiting incest and polygamy, with which I concur, though they are only abnormal conventionally and are not so damaging to a society biologically."

Both these men are leaders in just that community of thoughtful men and women I imagined; both have had and deserved highest honors as literary figures; and, while I believe one to be mistaken in his belief that sexual forthrightness is not a primary issue for the social good; and the other to be as misled by the unhappy conventions of his thought as by the atmosphere of guilty confession that he gathered from my essay; both, like I, are concerned not with the minority in question but rightly with what they consider the public good, an intimation of the human good. Much understanding yet is needed before men of good intentions can stand together.

[4]1959. I find myself in this passage accusing certain "critics," "poets," and "new cult leaders" of what I might be suspected of in my poetry myself. "Suffering, sensitivity, and magical quality" are constants of mood; divinities and cults, supernatural and visionary claims, and sexual mystery are all elements in subject matter that give rise to poetic inspiration for me. In recent years I have had an increased affinity with

the popular superstition, have accepted and even anticipated the charge of demonism. Sensing the fear in society that is generated in ignorance of their nature, they have sought not understanding but to live in terms of that ignorance, to become witch doctors in the modern chaos.

To go about this they have had to cover with mystery, to obscure the work of all those who have viewed homosexuality as but one of the many ways which human love may take and who have had primarily in mind as they wrote (as Melville, Proust, or Crane had) mankind and its liberation. For these great early artists their humanity was the source, the sole source, of their work. Thus in *Remembrance of Things Past,* Charlus is not seen as the special disintegration of a homosexual but as a human being in disintegration, and the forces that lead to that disintegration, the forces of pride, self-humiliation in love, jealousy, are not special forces but common to all men and women. Thus in Melville, though in *Billy Budd* it is clear that the conflict is homosexual, the forces that make for that conflict, the guilt in passion, the hostility rising from subconscious sources, and the sudden recognition of these forces as it comes to Vere in that story—these are forces which are universal, which rise in other contexts, which in Melville's work have risen in other contexts.

It is, however, the body of Crane that has been most ravaged by these modern ghouls and, once ravaged, stuck up cult-wise in the mystic light of their special cemetery literature. The live body of Crane is there, inviolate in the work; but in the window display of modern poetry, in so many special critics' and devotees' interest, is a painted mummy, deep sea green. One may tiptoe by, as the visi-

imaginative reaches of religious thought, searching gnostic and cabalistic speculation for a more diverse order.

The Demon of Moral Virtue exacts his dues wherever he is evoked. Where we seek the Good he urges us to substitute what will be men's good opinion of us. I may have felt then that I might redeem my sexuality as righteous in the sight of certain critics, if I disavowed my heterodoxy in religious imagination as wicked or deluded.

tors to Lenin's tomb tiptoe by, and, once outside, find themselves in a world in his name that has celebrated the defeat of all that he was devoted to. One need only point out in all the homosexual imagery of Crane, in the longing and vision of love, the absence of the private sensibility that colors so much of modern writing. Where the Zionists of homosexuality have laid claim to a Palestine of their own—asserting in their miseries their nationality; Crane's suffering, his rebellion and his love are sources of poetry for him, not because they are what makes him different from his fellowmen, but because he saw in them his link with mankind; he saw in them his share in universal human experience.5

What can one do in the face of this, both those critics and artists, not homosexual, who are, however, primarily concerned with dispelling all inhumanities, all forces of convention and law that impose a tyranny over man's nature, and those critics and artists

5 1959. The principal point is that the creative genius of a writer lies in his communication of personal experience as a communal experience. He brings us to realize our own inner being in a new light through the sense of human being he creates, or he creates in us as we read a new sense of our being. And in Melville, Crane, and Proust I saw their genius awaken a common share in homosexual desire and love, in its suffering and hope, that worked to transform the communal image of man.

Professors of literature do not always have minds of the same inspiration as the minds of writers whose work they interpret and evaluate for consumption; and an age of criticism has grown up to keep great spirits cut down to size so as to be of use in the self-esteem of sophisticated pusillanimous men in a continual self-improvement course. Thus Freud's courageous analysis of his motives and psychic dis-ease has furnished material for popular analysts like Fromm to be struck by how normal their psyches are compared to Freud's, how much more capable of mature love they are.

Homosexuality affords a ready point at which a respectable reader disassociates himself from the work of genius and seeks to avoid any sense of realizing his own inner being there. Some years after my essay, Leslie Fiedler, whom I take to be heterosexual, was able to gain some notoriety by writing about homosexual undercurrents in American literature, playing, not without a sense of his advantage, upon the cultural ambivalence between the appreciation of literature as a commodity of education and the depreciation of genius as it involves a new sense of being, and upon the sexual ambivalence in which the urbane American male can entertain the idea of homosexuality providing he is not responsible, providing he preserves his contempt for or his disavowal of sexual love between males.

who, as homosexuals, must face in their own lives both the hostility of society in that they are "queer" and the hostility of the homosexual élite in that they are merely human?

For the first group the starting point is clear, that they must recognize homosexuals as equals, and, as equals, allow them neither more nor less than can be allowed any human being. There are no special rights. For the second group the starting point is more difficult, the problem more treacherous.

In the face of the hostility of society which I risk in making even the acknowledgment explicit in this statement, in the face of the "crime" of my own feelings, in the past I publicized those feelings as private and made no stand for their recognition but tried to sell them as disguised, for instance, as conflicts arising from mystical sources.[6] I colored and perverted simple and direct emotions and realizations into a mysterious realm, a mysterious relation to society. Faced by the inhumanities of society I did not seek a solution in humanity but turned to a second outcast society as inhumane as the first. I joined those who, while they allowed for my sexual nature, allowed for so little of the moral, the sensible, and creative direction which all of living should reflect. They offered a family, outrageous as it was, a community in which one was not condemned for one's homosexuality, but it was necessary there for one to desert one's humanity, for which one would be suspect, "out of key. " In drawing rooms and in little magazines I celebrated the cult with a sense of sanctuary such as a medieval Jew must have found

[6] 1959. But there is no "explicit" statement here! What emerges is a "confession" (analyzed further below) instead of what was needed and what I was unable to say out. While I had found a certain acceptance in special circles of homosexuals and opportunities for what Kinsey calls "contacts," this was a travesty of what the heart longed for. I could not say "I am homosexual," because exactly this statement of minority identity was the lie. Our deepest sexuality is free and awakens toward both men and women where they are somehow akin to us. Perhaps the dawning realization that we are all exiles from paradise, and that somehow goods have their reality in that impossible dream where all men have come into their full nature, gave rise to and a thread of truth to the feeling of guilt that prompts this voice.

in the ghetto; my voice taking on the modulations which tell of the capitulation to snobbery and the removal from the "common sort"; my poetry exhibiting the objects made divine and tyrannical as the Catholic church has made bones of saints, and bread and wine tyrannical.[7]

[7] 1959. I am reminded in the foregoing passage of those confessions of duplicity, malice, and high treason made before the courts of Inquisition or the Moscow trials. "Society" appears as the merciless "hostile" judge; what I meant to avow—the profound good and even joyful life that might be realized in sexual love between men—becoming a confession that I had "disguised," "colored," "perverted," "celebrated the cult" and even in my work exhibited objects of alienation from the common law. Some remnant of Protestant adherence suggests there was Holy Roman wickedness, "divine and tyrannical as the Catholic Church has made."

Might there be a type of social reaction to which "confession" of "witches," "Trotskyites," and my confession as a "homosexual," conform? In the prototype there is first the volunteered list of crimes one has committed that anticipates the condemnaton of church or party or society. Then there is the fact that what one confesses as a social "crime" has been held somewhere as a hope and an ideal, contrary to convention. The heretic is guilty in his love or his righteousness because he has both the conventional common mind and the imagination of a new common mind; he holds in his own heart the adversary that he sees in the actual prosecutor. Often there was torture to bring on the confession, but it enacted the inner torture of divided mind. "Names cannot be named" I exclaim in this essay, and perhaps akin to that felt necessity is the third phase in which "witches" and "Trotskyites" eventually named their accomplices in heresy, throwing up their last allegiance to their complicity in hope.

This Jungian revival of alchemy with its doctrine of the *nigredo* and the related surrealistic cult of black humor or bile has complicated the contemporary sense of a belief that in some phase the psyche must descend against its nature into its adversary. It is an exciting idea just as a great destruction of the world by war is an exciting idea. Part of the force which "Beat" poets have is the authority which we give after Freud and Jung to the potency of crime.

"Being a junkie in America today," Ginsberg writes, "is like being a Jew in Nazi Germany." This leads to humorous comment, like the parody of Marx, that "Marijuana is the opium of the people," or that "Opium is the religion of the people." But the revelation of Ginsberg's formula is that in taking to junk he is trying to become like a Jew in Germany. He cannot realize in his Jewishness a sufficient extreme of persecution (even he cannot quite believe in racial guilt—the American idea of the melting pot as virtue is too strong). The "fuzz" cannot live up to the projection of wrath that might externalize inhibition as rank and unjust punishment and satisfy his guilt without calling his need to account. So he takes up "the angry fix." "Holy Burroughs" and heroin addiction will surely test the frustrating tolerance of a liberal state and reveal beneath the "Moloch whose breast is a cannibal dynamo."

After an evening at one of those salons where the whole atmosphere was one of suggestion and celebration, I returned recently experiencing again the aftershock, the desolate feeling of wrongness, remembering in my own voice and gestures the rehearsal of unfeeling. Alone, not only I, but, I felt, the others who had appeared as I did so mocking, so superior in feeling, had known, knew still, those troubled emotions, the deep and integral longings that we as human beings feel, holding us from archaic actions by the powerful sense of humanity that is their source, longings that lead us to love, to envision a creative life. "Towards something far," as Hart Crane wrote, "now farther away than ever."

Among those who should understand those emotions which society condemned, one found that the group language did not allow for any feeling at all other than this self-ridicule, this "gaiety" (it is significant that the homosexual's word for his own kind is "gay"), a wave surging forward, breaking into laughter and then receding, leaving a wake of disillusionment, a disbelief that extends to oneself, to life itself. What then, disowning this career, can one turn to?

What I think can be asserted as a starting point is that only one devotion can be held by a human being seeking a creative life and expression, and that is a devotion to human freedom, toward the liberation of human love, human conflicts, human aspirations. To do this one must disown *all* the special groups (nations, churches, sexes, races) that would claim allegiance. To hold this devotion every written word, every spoken word, every action, every purpose must be examined and considered. The old fears, the old specialties will be there, mocking and tempting; the old protective associations will be there, offering for a surrender of one's humanity congratulation upon one's special nature and value. It must be always recognized that the others, those who have surrendered their humanity, are not less than oneself. It must be always remembered that one's own honesty, one's battle against the inhumanity of his own group (be it against patriotism, against bigotry, against—in this special case—the homosexual cult) is a battle that cannot be won in the immediate scene. The forces of inhumanity are overwhelming, but only one's continued opposition can make any other order possible, will give an added strength for all those who desire freedom and equality to break at last those fetters that seem now so unbreakable.

REFLECTIONS 1959

In the fifteen years since the writing of "The Homosexual in Society," my circumstances have much changed. Life and my work have brought me new friends, where the community of values is more openly defined, and even, in recent years, a companion who shares my concern for a creative life. Distressed where I have been distressed and happy where I have been happy, their sympathy has rendered absurd whatever apprehension I had concerning the high moral resolve and radical reformation of character needed before I would secure recognition and understanding. It is a kinship of concern and a sharing of experience that draws us together.

The phantasmic idea of a "society" that was somehow hostile, the sinister affiliation offered by groups with whom I had no common ground other than the specialized sexuality, the anxiety concerning the good opinion of the community—all this sense of danger remains, for I am not a person of reserved nature; and conventional morality, having its roots in Judaic tribal law and not in philosophy, holds homosexual relations to be a crime. Love, art, and thought are all social goods for me; and often I must come, where I would begin a friendship, to odd moments of trial and doubts when I must deliver account of my sexual nature that there be no mistake in our trust.

But the inspiration of the essay was toward something else, a public trust, larger and more demanding than the respect of friends. To be respected as a member of the political community for what one knew in one's heart to be respectable! To insist, not upon tolerance for a divergent sexual practice, but upon concern for the virtues of a homosexual relationship! I was, I think, at the threshold

of a critical concept: sexual love wherever it was taught and prac-
ticed was a single adventure, that troubadours sang in romance,
that poets have kept as a traditional adherence, and that novelists
have given scope. Love is dishonored where sexual love between
those of the same sex is despised; and where love is dishonored
there is no public trust.

It is my sense that the fulfillment of man's nature lies in the
creation of that trust; and where the distrusting imagination sets
up an image of "self" against the desire for unity and mutual sympathy, the state called "Hell" is created. There we find the visceral
agonies, sexual aversions and possessions, excitations and depres-
sions, the omnipresent "I" that bears true witness to its condition
in "Howl" or "Kaddish," in McClure's *Hymns to St. Geryon* or the
depressive "realism" of Lowell's *Life Studies*. "We are come to the
place," Virgil tells Dante as they enter Hell, "where I told thee thou
shouldst see the wretched people, who have lost the good of the
intellect." In Hell, the homosexuals go, as Dante rightly saw them,
as they still go often in the streets of our cities, looking "as in the
evening men are wont to look at one another under a new moon,"
running beneath the hail of a sharp torment, having wounds, recent
and old, where the flames of experience have burned their bodies.

It is just here, when he sees his beloved teacher, Brunetto Latini,
among the sodomites, that Dante has an inspired intuition that goes
beyond the law of his church and reaches toward a higher ethic:
"Were my desire all fulfilled," he says to Brunetto, "you had not yet
been banished from human nature: for in my memory is fixed . . . the
dear and kind, paternal image of you, when in the world, hour by
hour, you taught me how man makes himself eternal. . . ."

"Were my desire all fulfilled . . ." springs from the natural heart
in the confidence of its feelings that has often been more generous than conventions and institutions. I picture that fulfillment of
desire as a human state of mutual volition and aid, a shared life.

Not only in sexual love, but in work and in play, we suffer from the dominant competitive ethos which gives rise to the struggle of interests to gain recognition or control, and discourages the recognition of the needs and interests which we all know we have in common. Working for money (and then, why not stealing or cheating for money?) is the "realistic" norm, and working for the common good is the "idealistic" exception. "I have always earned my living at manual labor," an old friend writes. And his voice breaks through, like a shaft of sunlight through an industrial smog, the oppressive voices of junkies and pushers, petty thieves and remittance men of social security with their need and misery set adrift of itself. Oppressive, because these are sensitive young men and women I am thinking of, some of them the artists and poets of a new generation.

The sense of this essay rests then upon the concept that sexual love between those of the same sex is one with sexual love between men and women; and that this love is one of the conditions of the fulfillment of the heart's desire and the restoration of man's free nature. Creative work for the common good is one of the conditions of that nature. And our hope lies still in the creative imagination wherever it unifies what had been thought divided, wherever it transforms the personal experience into a communal good, "that Brunetto Latini had not been banished from human nature."

TWO POEMS BY HART CRANE

Legend

As silent as a mirror is believed
Realities plunge in silence by . . .

I am not ready for repentance;
Nor to match regrets. For the moth
Bends no more than the still
Imploring flame. And tremorous
In the white falling flakes
Kisses are, —
The only worth all granting.

It is to be learned—
This cleaving and this burning,
But only by the one who
Spends out himself again.

Twice and twice
(Again the smoking souvenir,
Bleeding eidolon!) and yet again.
Until the bright logic is won
Unwhispering as a mirror
Is believed.

Then, drop by caustic drop, a perfect cry
Shall string some constant harmony,—
Relentless caper for all those who step
The legend of their youth into the noon.

To Brooklyn Bridge

How many dawns, chill from his rippling rest
The seagull's wings shall dip and pivot him,
Shedding white rings of tumult, building high
Over the chained bay waters Liberty—

Then, with inviolate curve, forsake our eyes
As apparitional as sails that cross
Some page of figures to be filed away;
—Till elevators drop us from our day . . .

I think of cinemas, panoramic sleights
With multitudes bent toward some flashing scene
Never disclosed, but hastened to again,
Foretold to other eyes on the same screen;

And Thee, across the harbor, silver-paced
As though the sun took step of thee, yet left
Some motion ever unspent in thy stride, —
Implicitly thy freedom staying thee!

Out of some subway scuttle, cell or loft
A bedlamite speeds to thy parapets,
Tilting there momently, shrill shirt ballooning,
A jest falls from the speechless caravan.

Down Wall, from girder into street noon leaks,
A rip-tooth of the sky's acetylene;
All afternoon the cloud-flown derricks turn . . .
Thy cables breathe the North Atlantic still.

And obscure as that heaven of the Jews,
Thy guerdon . . . Accolade thou dost bestow
Of anonymity time cannot raise:
Vibrant reprieve and pardon thou dost show.

O harp and altar, of the fury fused,
(How could mere toil align thy choiring strings!)
Terrific threshold of the prophet's pledge,
Prayer of pariah, and the lover's cry,—

Again the traffic lights that skim thy swift
Unfractioned idiom, immaculate sigh of stars,
Beading thy path—condense eternity:
And we have seen night lifted in thine arms.

Under thy shadow by the piers I waited;
Only in darkness is thy shadow clear.
The City's fiery parcels all undone,
Already snow submerges an iron year . . .

O Sleepless as the river under thee,
Vaulting the sea, the prairies' dreaming sod,
Unto us lowliest sometime sweep, descend
And of the curveship lend a myth to God.

TWO POEMS BY WALT WHITMAN

To You

Whoever you are, I fear you are walking the walks of dreams,
I fear these supposed realities are to melt from under your feet
and hands,
Even now your features, joys, speech, house, trade, manners,
troubles, follies, costume, crimes, dissipate away from you,
Your true soul and body appear before me.
They stand forth out of affairs, out of commerce, shops, work,
farms, clothes, the house, buying, selling, eating, drinking,
suffering, dying.

Whoever you are, now I place my hand upon you, that you be
my poem,
I whisper with my lips close to your ear.
I have loved many women and men, but I love none better than
you.

O I have been dilatory and dumb,
I should have made my way straight to you long ago,
I should have blabb'd nothing but you, I should have chanted
nothing but you.

I will leave all and come and make the hymns of you,
None has understood you, but I understand you,
None has done justice to you, you have not done justice to
yourself,
None but has found you imperfect, I only find no imperfection in
you,

None but would subordinate you, I only am he who will never
    consent to subordinate you,
I only am he who places over you no master, owner, better, God,
    beyond what waits intrinsically in yourself.

Painters have painted their swarming groups and the centre-
    figure of all,
From the head of the centre-figure spreading a nimbus of gold-
    color'd light,
But I paint myriads of heads, but paint no head without its
    nimbus of gold-color'd light,
From my hand from the brain of every man and woman it
    streams, effulgently flowing forever.

O I could sing such grandeurs and glories about you!
You have not known what you are, you have slumber'd upon
    yourself all your life,
Your eyelids have been the same as closed most of the time,
What you have done returns already in mockeries,
(Your thrift, knowledge, prayers, if they do not return in
    mockeries, what is their return?)

The mockeries are not you,
Underneath them and within them I see you lurk,
I pursue you where none else has pursued you,
Silence, the desk, the flippant expression, the night, the
    accustom'd routine, if these conceal you from others or from
    yourself, they do not conceal you from me,
The shaved face, the unsteady eye, the impure complexion, if
    these balk others they do not balk me,
The pert apparel, the deform'd attitude, drunkenness, greed,
    premature death, all these I part aside.

There is no endowment in man or woman that is not tallied in you,
There is no virtue, no beauty in man or woman, but as good is in
    you,
No pluck, no endurance in others, but as good is in you,
No pleasure waiting for others, but an equal pleasure waits for
    you.

As for me, I give nothing to any one except I give the like
    carefully to you,
I sing the songs of the glory of none, not God, sooner than I sing
    the songs of the glory of you.

Whoever you are! claim your own at any hazard!
These shows of the East and West are tame compared to you,
These immense meadows, these interminable rivers, you are
    immense and interminable as they,
These furies, elements, storms, motions of Nature, throes of
    apparent dissolution, you are he or she who is master or
    mistress over them,
Master or mistress in your own right over Nature, elements,
    pain, passion, dissolution.

The hopples fall from your ankles, you find an unfailing
    sufficiency,
Old or young, male or female, rude, low, rejected by the rest,
    whatever you are promulges itself,
Through birth, life, death, burial, the means are provided,
    nothing is scanted,
Through angers, losses, ambition, ignorance, ennui, what you are
    picks its way.

Give Me the Splendid Silent Sun

I

Give me the splendid silent sun with all his beams full-dazzling,
Give me autumnal fruit ripe and red from the orchard,
Give me a field where the unmow'd grass grows,
Give me an arbor, give me the trellis'd grape,
Give me fresh corn and wheat, give me serene-moving animals
    teaching content,
Give me nights perfectly quiet as on high plateaus west of the
Mississippi, and I looking up at the stars,
Give me odorous at sunrise a garden of beautiful flowers where I
    can walk undisturb'd,
Give me for marriage a sweet-breath'd woman of whom I should
    never tire,
Give me a perfect child, give me away aside from the noise of the
    world a rural domestic life,
Give me to warble spontaneous songs recluse by myself, for my
    own ears only,
Give me solitude, give me Nature, give me again O Nature your
    primal sanities!

These demanding to have them, (tired with ceaseless excitement,
    and rack'd by the war-strife,)
These to procure incessantly asking, rising in cries from my heart,
While yet incessantly asking still I adhere to my city,
Day upon day and year upon year O city, walking your streets,
Where you hold me enchain'd a certain time refusing to give me up,
Yet giving to make me glutted, enrich'd of soul, you give me
    forever faces;
(O I see what I sought to escape, confronting, reversing my cries,
    see my own soul trampling down what it ask'd for.)

2

Keep your splendid silent sun,
    Keep your woods O Nature, and the quiet places by the
    woods,
Keep your fields of clover and timothy, and your corn-fields and
    orchards,
Keep the blossoming buckwheat fields where the Ninth-month
    bees hum;
Give me faces and streets--give me these phantoms incessant and
    endless along the trottoirs!
Give me interminable eyes--give me women--give me comrades
    and lovers by the thousand!
Let me see new ones every day--let me hold new ones by the hand
    every day!
Give me such shows--give me the streets of Manhattan!
Give me Broadway, with the soldiers marching--give me the
    sound of the trumpets and drums!
(The soldiers in companies or regiments--some starting away,
    flush'd and reckless,
Some, their time up, returning with thinn'd ranks, young, yet
    very old, worn, marching, noticing nothing;)
Give me the shores and wharves heavy-fringed with black ships!
O such for me! O an intense life, full to repletion and varied!
The life of the theatre, bar-room, huge hotel, for me!
The saloon of the steamer! the crowded excursion for me! the
    torchlight procession!
The dense brigade bound for the war, with high piled military
    wagons following;
People, endless, streaming, with strong voices, passions, pageants,
Manhattan streets with their powerful throbs, with beating
    drums as now,

The endless and noisy chorus, the rustle and clank of muskets,
    (even the sight of the wounded,)
Manhattan crowds, with their turbulent musical chorus!
Manhattan faces and eyes forever for me.

THREE POEMS
BY TENNESSEE WILLIAMS

As I Stood in My Room Tonight

As I stood in my room tonight, drinking a solitary toast
to the great poet of all time, Hart Crane,
I began to dance.

For in the distance I heard a radio playing.

I was in Brooklyn, in view of the Bridge,
I could see it from my seventeenth story window.

I saw you stride across it, Hart, great, swinging stars
with lanterns in both hands.

A bellowing voice! O you were the giant of Brooklyn,
I saw you followed by companies of sailors,

Whitman came after you, too, spewing wine on his beard,
Poe with his raven followed at some distance.

Unholy Trinity!

But there was fellowship in you.

You stood, Crane, on the Bridge and shouted to Melville,
I heard his hollow answer from the deep.

So many swimmers sprang, so many fish!
The air was cut by wings of phosphorescence,

Beneath arcades the hearty loiterers tossed silver coins,
O I, I danced with them, too, on my seventeenth story,

I was filled with the running warmth, the greatness of blood
which is you, dear Brawling Crane!

Recuerdo

1. THE BLOODLESS VIOLETS

And he remembered the death of his grandmother
whose hands were accustomed to draw white curtains about him
before he moved to Electric Avenue . . .

In childhood's spectrum of violence, she remained pale,
a drift of linen among tall, sunny chambers.

It was not ordained by God, nor any minister of Him,
that time should be caught in the withered crook of her elbow
or that she who would not
                              give injury to birds,
had nevertheless been called upon to carry
a cage full of swallows into an evil guest chamber

because her hands,
                    the knuckles of which were arthritic,
                    finger tips numbed by winter,
could not disengage
          the long-ago hairpin twisted about the cage door . . .

But Spring's first almost bloodless violets were removed
from the washing machine in the basement,
                    making it plain
          why such a contagion of languor,
                    brought indoors with the laundry,
made visitors yawn.

Possibly also explaining why slumber's mischievous matchmaking
had put him to bed with young witches,
    indistinct beings anonymous of gender,
      some of them only a hollowness fastened upon his
        groin
and drawing, drawing,
    the jelly out of his bones and leaving him only,
      finally,
        tenderly,
          coldly —
the damp initial of Eros.

2. EPISODE

And then the long, long peltering schools of rain!

    Ozzie, the black nurse,
      tussles with the awnings,
        a peppery kind of battle
in which she is worsted.
        — Lightning,
          her starched white skirt,
is yanked across heaven!
    Aw, God, Mizz Williams!
  —horse liniment stung her,
And in the morning,
      a telephone pole in our attic,
    slippery, blanched —
    A Mississippi tornado!

3. THE PAPER LANTERN

My sister was quicker at everything than I.

At five she could say the multiplication tables
        with barely a pause for breath,
        while I was employed
with frames of colored beads in Kindy Garden.

At eight she could play
                Idillio and The Scarf Dance
while I was chopping at scales and exercises.

At fifteen my sister
                no longer waited for me,
impatiently at the White Star Pharmacy corner
        but plunged headlong
        into the discovery, Love!

Then vanished completely —

for love's explosion, defined as early madness,
consumingly shone in her transparent heart for a season
and burned it out, a tissue-paper lantern!

                — torn from a string!
                — tumbled across a pavilion!

flickering three times, almost seeming to cry . . .
My sister was quicker at everything than I.

The Beanstalk Country

You know how the mad come into a room,
too boldly,
their eyes exploding on the air like roses,
their entrances from space we never entered.
They're always attended by someone small and friendly
who goes between their awful world and ours
as though explaining but really only smiling,
a snowy gull that dips above a wreck.

They see not us, nor any Sunday caller
among the geraniums and wicker chairs,
for they are Jacks who climb the beanstalk country,
a place of hammers and tremendous beams,
compared to which the glassed solarium
in which we rise to greet them has no light.

The news we bring them, common, reassuring,
drenched with the cheerful idiocy of noon,
cannot compete with what they have to tell
of what they saw through cracks in the ogre's oven.

And we draw back. The snowy someone says,
Don't mind their talk, they are disturbed today!

A POEM BY E. E. CUMMINGS

somewhere i have never travelled,gladly beyond
any experience,your eyes have their silence:
in your most frail gesture are things which enclose me,
or which i cannot touch because they are too near

your slightest look will easily unclose me
though i have closed myself as fingers,
you open always petal by petal myself as Spring opens
touching skilfully,mysteriously)her first rose

or if your wish be to close me, i and
my life will shut very beautifully ,suddenly,
as when the heart of this flower imagines
the snow carefully everywhere descending;

nothing which we are to perceive in this world equals
the power of your intense fragility:whose texture
compels me with the color of its countries,
rendering death and forever with each breathing

(i do not know what it is about you that closes
and opens;only something in me understands
the voice of your eyes is deeper than all roses)
nobody,not even the rain,has such small hands